Peter Sloan Teaches HTML Programming

Web Documents, Graphics And Credit Card Payment Links

by Peter Julius Sloan

Printed in April, 2012 by
Sloans Book Press
New York City, NY
10036

ISBN-13: 978-1470141233
ISBN: 1-47014123X

Table of Contents

Introduction: Learn HTML Programming – Before and After

Tired of your ads looking like this?

Ho Dums, Call us. You will get the best price guaranteed. We beat all prices for our services (no doubt), Best repair, best service, money back but only if you can beat our price. We got the best people on staff. You will get what you paid for. Trust us; we is not a scam. Please pay us $200. We have no money. Call us a peace out.

Or even the tacky guy that paid a one time fee to hire a graphic designer but you know his ad only goes to one place, an outsourcing person who does not give any extra work to his local people. You can tell by the pixels and blurriness that this is not well done.

And turn your ad into one that looks like this...

Ho Dums Home Repair, Licensed Contractors
888-888-1154

Ho Dums Home Repair.LLC
New York, NY

$200 down

Hourly Rate: $ 20.00 per hour

Price Details: Flat Fee as well

Description:

Publication Printing, Web & Graphic Design, Computer Repair, Flyers, Logos, Custom Business Cards

Office: 888-888-1154
Call Or Text Our Cell: 888-888-6767
Email: sales@HoDumsHomeRepair.com

This book covers everything from custom coding your HTML code, adding in links, graphics, banners, forms and even more of the business side of view such as registering your LLC, getting your Tax ID, a licensed business phone, business email and even a google voice mail and the works and even your web site with your custom domain name.

This all starts by admitting one simple bit of truth, you current ad needs help and you do not even have 20% of the income you are supposed to. Where did I learn to make ads better? I started out as a New York City Kids and passed talent portfolio reviews at a young age to be accepted to Brooklyn Museum art school, move on to the High School of Art and Design and do a Bachelors in Fine Arts concentrating in Graphic Design and New Media as well as a Masters of System Administration in getting all of my devices working properly to operate my business as a commercial artist.

One of the first things we look out for is a page of artwork or text that does not have anything going on and work on getting the elements of the page to look more artistic and dynamically done.

From the before or after you saw every single week at your home office should be a 10K of sales at your own desk processing credit cards over the phone while filling your appointment book with tons of callers. By graphic designing your classified ad to look better and get a business set up you can do all of these things. The way it is going for you, being caught operating a business without a Tax ID, you stand to be arrested and dragged to your local town court and tried. The charges can be anything from operating without a license to evading taxes to any number of things. Get your classified ad and web site working properly and you will see tons of new clients and streams of extra income.

Peter Julius Sloan
A+, Net+, MCP
S.U.N.Y. Purchase Class of 2003, F.I.D.E. 2230
Department of Education Chess & Dell 2003 - 2008

Chapter 1: Getting Licensed

You can get licensed in any trade whether it be real estate, financial products, medical, information technology, teaching, loans, security, contracting, legal, even customer service. I have one from CompTIA which makes me certified in customer service for computers parts and devices. For those of us who are looking for a more artistic license, get a degree in liberal arts, fine arts, history or mathematics. Of course, these degrees require higher education and can be very expensive, they help make peoples lives more fulfilling.

Here is a route I had to follow to get up my classified ad. While I already had a Bachelors of Fine Arts and was running a classified ad in Graphic Designer, I had a lot of clients say they were not interested because that is just school, and not work experience. I had to go back and get certified as an I.T. which relieved most of my client's concerns that I was good with using the computer systems as a certified professional. I noticed that this did not help with any of my work with print publishing or web design so I took an extra year of course work to become a Microsoft Office Specialist. Only after this point did I get more of a regular client pool as well as a steady stream of temp assignments with my pay rate being over $25 per hour. You must get a license to successfully conduct a business in your state.

I had a few friends who took up a federal business opportunity offering modifications to people that were late on their mortgages, but even though they were only working to help people out and no license was required, the office kept getting a call from a party asking to show their license. Robert furnished his attorney and legal aid licenses and Alex had many broker licenses going back to even cold calling for a stock brokerage. Their business was permitted to operate. Having a license is the only way to get ahead and have a steady stream of income.

Chapter 2: Getting A Tax ID, Business Phone And PayPal Business Account

Getting a Tax ID is easy these days, just go to www.IRS.gov and search or *'Apply for an Employer Identification Number (EIN) Online'.* You will be directed to the online form that will ask you a few short questions and you will be given your EIN right over the internet.

EIN Assistant

Important Information Before You Begin

Use this assistant to apply for and obtain an Employer Identification Number (EIN).
Do I need an EIN?
Do I need a new EIN?

> For help or additional information on any topic, click the underlined key words, or view Help Topics on the right side of the screen. Make sure that pop-ups are allowed from this site.

About the EIN Assistant

- You must complete this application in one session, as you will **not** be able to save and return at a later time.
- For security purposes, your session will expire after 15 minutes of inactivity, and you will need to start over.
- You will receive your EIN immediately upon verification. When will I be able to use my EIN?
- If you wish to receive your confirmation letter online, we strongly recommended that you install Adobe Reader before beginning the application if it is not already installed.

Restrictions

- Due to a high volume of requests for EINs, the IRS will begin limiting the number of EINs assigned per day to a responsible party. Effective April 11, a responsible party will be limited to five (5) EINs in one business day. This limit is in effect whether you apply online, by phone, fax or mail.
- If a third party designee (TPD) is completing the online application on behalf of the taxpayer, the taxpayer must authorize the third party to apply for and receive the EIN on his or her behalf.
- The business location must be within the United States or U.S. territories.
- Foreign filers without an Individual Taxpayer Identification Number (ITIN) cannot use this assistant to obtain an EIN.
- If you were incorporated outside of the United States or the U.S. territories, you cannot apply for an EIN online. Please call us at 267-941-1099 (this is not a toll free number).

Begin Application >>

If you are not comfortable sending information via the Internet, download the Form SS-4 PDF file and the instructions for alternative ways of applying.

Make sure you save your EIN in a secure place and print out a copy for your records. Wait we are not done yet. You must validate your EIN with your state tax office. This costs a small fee between $85 and up depending on which state. Validation takes a few weeks and your new sales tax certificate will come in the mail. The very first quarter I had my EIN I did not file my state taxes statement online and got a $50 fine. Make sure you file your sales tax quarterly, the quarters ending in March 1st, June 1st, September 1st and December 1st.

Now that we have our EIN we are going to get a business phone. Many phone companies start off with a form that asks for an EIN to be able to open a business account. All of the phone company web sites start off with a page similar to below asking to state if your are a personal user or business.

Personal	Small Business	Enterprise Business

When signing up for business you will be asked a series of questions to open an account. This consists of owning your own company and stating that you are the owner of the EIN and authorized to use it for new phone service. Many companies will require you fax in a confirmation of your sales tax certificate as well as your drivers license but that is all. There is a credit check involved but a short brief one that only takes a second and almost everyone is approved.

Tip: Only go for a credit check with a company that you are already approved with. I had Sprint for years before I upgraded to business. Would T-mobile approve me, most likely not, so I settled my old account and put them on the do not call list. Go with a company you already use and trust.

Opening a Merchant Account or PayPal Business account is relatively simple and involves a few easy steps. You must provide the following information in your application:

1. Name
2. Driver License Number
3. Business Name
4. Business Address (make it the same one as on your tax certificate)
5. Tax ID #

You will have to sign under perjury affirming that the Tax ID is yours and not someone else's. Just get your own Tax ID, EIN in the steps I showed above. That makes you a company owner and the owner of a small to mid size property.

That's it; you are done. You will get instant approval over the phone. Once again, get approved by a company you already work with. I had an eBay and PayPal account going all the way back to 1999 and did not apply for a virtual terminal for some years later. If PayPal says no, getting one at your bank is the easiest way to go, or even upgrading your Amazon Payments account to business with a few easy steps involved. A merchant account with a bank includes a credit check for a history of paying charge backs. I built up my credit history with PayPal paying back damages caused by store thieves. Paying back negative balances all goes on your business credit to become a merchant. Paying on time even better; you can become a small size department store operating your sales business out of your own home office with no boss to ever tell you when to get to work or to punch your time sheet. You will be an independent small business owner and free to work when you choose.

Chapter 3: Formatting Text & Tables In HTML

There are two standard programs for formatting text for HTML. The first one of course is Microsoft Word which not only formats text but also has features to allow you to save your Word documents as web documents. The second is DreamWeaver which is the industry standard for designing web sites. While we can make the best charts and diagrams using Word, DreamWeaver allows us to take templates from sources such as www.ThemeForrest.com, quickly edit them and get them uploaded onto your web hosting service with any of a number of companies, the hottest one out there today being GoDaddy. For how to edit web site templates using Microsoft Online, Google Sites, or GoDaddy Web Sites Tonight, see Chapter 10: Working With Templates.

There are two ways to insert text, the first is a text box and the second is text on the page or in the table. While Word and DreamWeaver will both primarily insert to text straight onto the page, there are other features which allow using layers. Layers are a very big problem with different browsers viewing the layers in different ways. The extra plug-in required is Java Script and this has a different appearance in every single computer you will use so we are going to stick with the way I teach this to all of my students, by creating tables, dividing the tables into different sub tables with various different columns and rows, and then inserting the text when we are ready.

Here we are starting with one table inserted at 100%. In Word Click Table/ Insert/ Table/ A dialogue box will pop-up asking you how many rows and columns as well as table size and for extra options such as background color.

We will start with this 2 columns and 8 rows table. I chose a standard 2 columns table for my navigation to be on the left and 8 rows because my web site has 7 categories with the topmost left corner reserved for my logo.

If your web site has only 4 or 5 categories reserve the extra row for a top left image or logo, which is industry standard these days. Larger web sites requiring sub categories you can find in Chapter 9.

Now we are going to merge all of the rows in the right column except for the topmost row. Hold down your mouse cursor starting at the bottom of the table inside the bottom cell and click and drag upwards until all of the cells in the right row are highlighted except for the topmost row. Click Table/ Merge Cells. You will have now one area for the body and the left column for your categories.

Click and drag the center dividing line to the left and make the main body of the page at least 80% of what you are looking at.

Now we are going to insert the logo in the top left corner. Place your mouse into the top leftmost cell and click Insert/ Picture/ From File. Browse to the directory where you keep your images, in my case under my user name psloan2001/My Pictures using Windows 7.

Tips On Images: Make sure your images are in jpeg or gif format. You cannot use vector or postscript images. Get your images into the correct format using Microsoft Office Picture Manager which comes with your Microsoft Office Professional and is located in your Microsoft Office tools folder. I also have a license for Adobe Photoshop which can be purchased on Adobe.com for a one time fee and the license you can keep for life. A colleague at school often recommended Paint Shop Pro for users that cannot afford Adobe which is expensive. Get a copy of Paint Shop and retouch all of your images. Unfortunately, Microsoft Paint does not do the job, but only saves the images as .bmp or .png and does not allow cropping. You must at least find a copy of Paint Shop to get your images working.

Now we are continuing by adding in our copyrighted title and text. I save all of my copyright material on a DVD and backup drive and keep them very organized, with my latest copyright registration arriving in the mail, with my slogan and content as well as my keywords all pressed by the Library of Congress Washington D.C. File your copyrights online at www.CopyRight.gov The fee is only $35. This is very important when you leave your material hanging out on the web for readers to copy and paste it into other sites and say it is theirs. Take it from me, being a young man back some years ago my old artwork portfolio web site www.ChessArtist.com was up on the web for over three years when I suddenly got a email from N-Vidia (who is a graphics card company that sponsors me) telling me I may have to remove some of my original artwork before these guys that stole my copyright file suit. Absolutely register your copyright before or at least have it copyright pending while your work is on the web.

So before we were so rudely interrupted my the copy thieves, we will now copy and paste in our text into the top right cell displaying our company name as well as slogan. Also, paste in the names of your tables on the left hand side. I add my phone number to every button to assure the client can reach me. Make the title of your web page bigger than your slogan to make sure your company name is visible. This is done with the regular text formatting features in Word by clicking on point size, choosing a nice size like 22 points, making the color lime green and choosing bold. Last but not least, add your phone number into the extra space below the title and slogan and put it in nice 36 point text. We are in a deals closing business, people. If the reader cannot find our phone number, then that is a customer out the door and not coming back.

	SloanTeaches.com
	Add your site slogan 'Sloan' here Who What Sloan? Peter Julius Sloan
	# 347-451-1154

Certificates 347-451-1154	
Teaching DOE 347-451-1154	
Freelance 347-451-1154	
Wait Staff 347-451-1154	
Casino 347-451-1154	
Copyright 347-451-1154	
Contact Us 347-451-1154	

Now we will make all of the buttons in the left hand table into hyper links. They must all lead to pages such as SloanTeaches.com/Certificates.aspx SloanTeaches.com/Teaching.aspx SloanTeaches.com/Freelance.aspx SloanTeaches.com/WaitStaff.aspx SloanTeaches.com/Casino.aspx SloanTeaches.com/Copyright.aspx SloanTeaches.com/ContactUs.aspx The links are added through the following steps.

Highlight the text you would like to link, right mouse click select Hyperlink and the following window will pop-up.

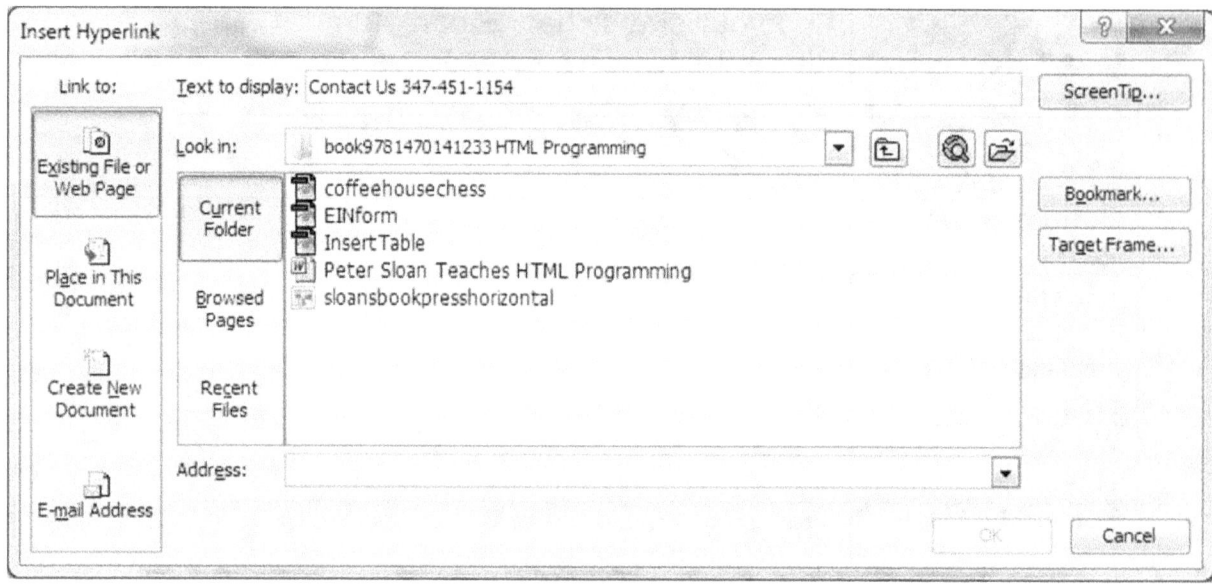

In the address field type in, or better yet copy and paste, your hyperlink and click OK. You will now have a hyperlink to your web address. Repeat these steps for all of the buttons in the left table until your task is complete and all of the buttons are created.

Question from the readers: Ok great hyperlinks and navigation, but get to the juicy stuff. We already bought Photoshop and need to know how to make our buttons into jpeg or gif images?

No sweat. Follow these steps. I am a detailed person and make many web sites from scratch, so follow me on this. Write down all the names of your 7 buttons on a scrap of paper.

Now open Adobe Photoshop and Click File/ New. The following dialogue box will pop-up.

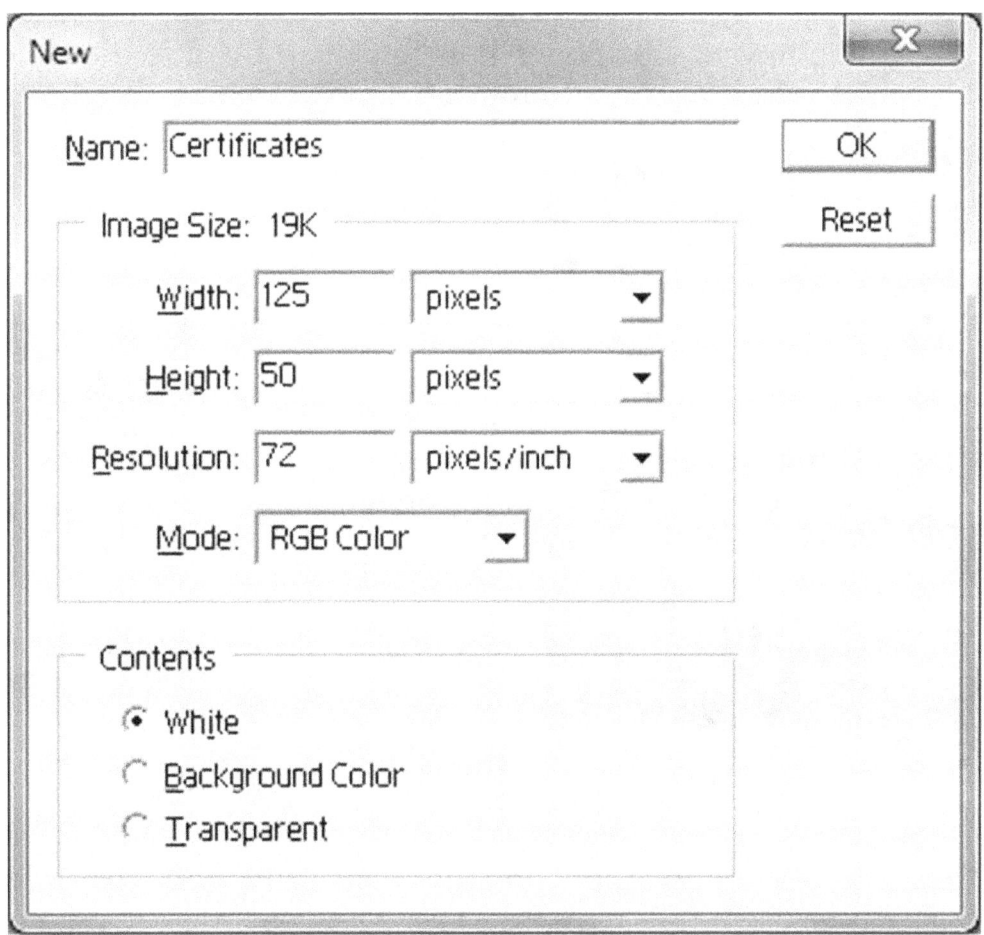

Give the document the same name as your button, specify the Width and Height make the resolution 72 pixels per inch and make the mode RGB color. For contents select Transparent background which is recommended for web images especially gif's.

On your Toolbar select the text tool which is the T symbol.

Choose your text color by clicking in the square indicated on the Right arrow shown below. Also choose your font and point size.

Add in your text phone number. Align them to the center.
Use the arrow key to move the text to be centered on the page.

Certificates
347-451-1154

Add in a nice background image. I am recommending a nice neutral color grey or blue like clouds. I found mine by going to Microsoft.com Clip Art & Media located in the Office section of the web site or Google.com/images and searching for the keyword of the image you would like to add.

Certificates
347-451-1154

Tip On Using Photoshop Layers: You may have noticed at the end of the previous example that our background image was pasted behind the text. This is done with layers. The layers window is shown below and you can add new layers by clicking on Insert/ New/ Layer and the following dialogue box will pop-up.

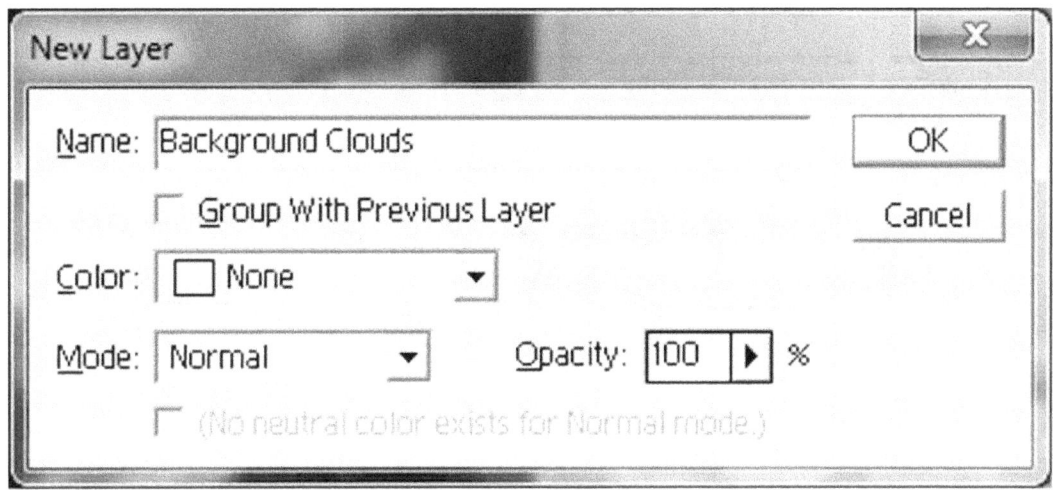

Give your layer a name, mine was Background Clouds. Mode/ Normal Opacity 100% but you can play with this to change it up for different effects.

While this background layer is locked from making changes you can move it to your other document by clicking in Select/ All then click Edit/ Copy and moving over to the other document. Then click Edit/ Paste. Once your background goes into its own layer, you are all set and ready to save your image for the web.

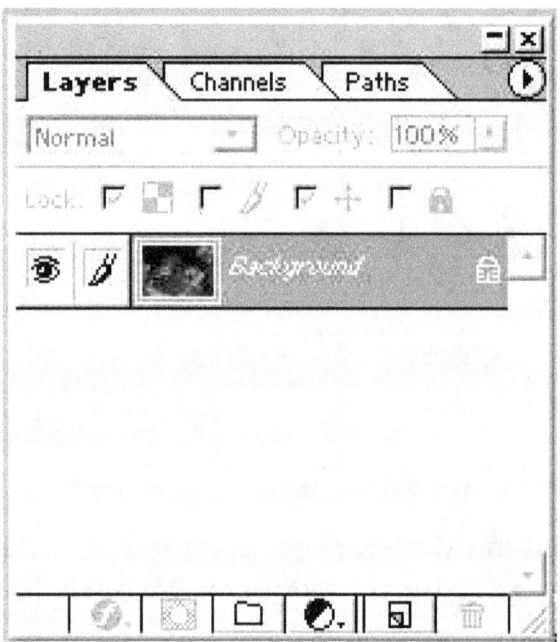

By creating a new layer and copy and pasting your image into the new document you will get rid of the lock and be able to make changes in your new document. Repeat these steps for the rest of your buttons, creating each button one at a time.

Question from the reader: I copy and pasted my images together and added my text. Are the images ready for the web yet?

Not yet: we must use Adobe Photoshop's patent protected Save for Web feature located under the File menu. Once you have your document the way you want it for your web site, click File/ Save for Web

The following screen will pop-up. I recommend staying in the default optimized view, clicking on the image tab and specifying the pixel size you would like to use. Keep the quality high as with current day high speed internet and bandwidth, you do not need to compress with low quality any more.

Once typing in your pixel sizes in the following part of the screen, for the table we made, the Width should be no more than 125 pixels and you can set your own height.

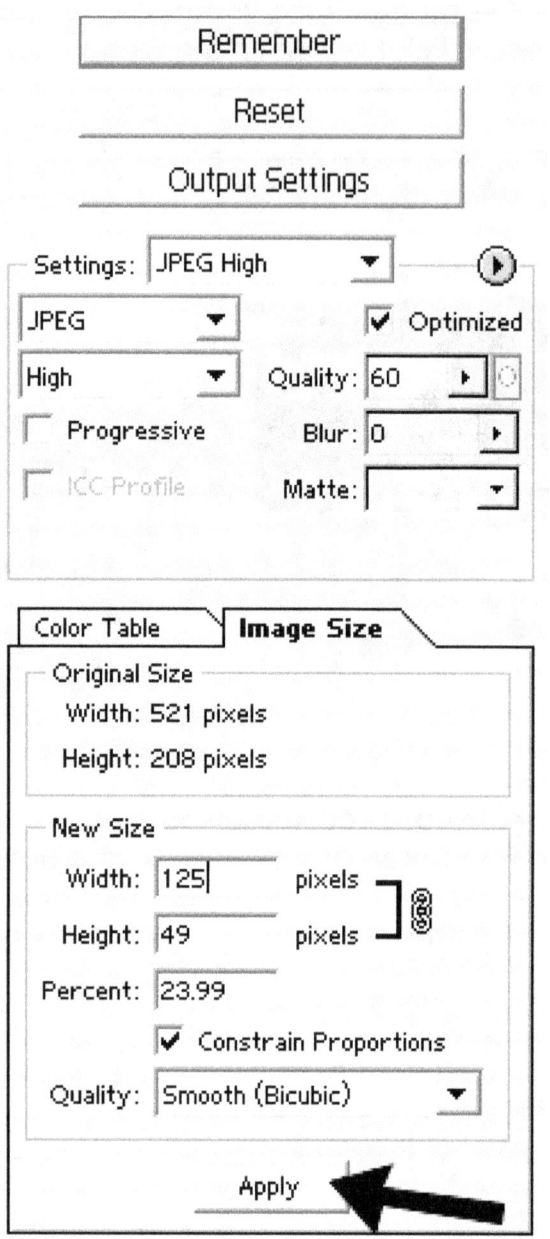

Click Apply where the arrow is shown above. Click Save, give your image a name and you are done. Your image is ready for the web.

Question from the readers: Ok, we typed in our phone number on the top banner just like you said but want to add one that looks more like a car commercial or real estate ad billboard size numbers and digits. Can you guide us through the steps?

The answer is yes, I did the same thing because I was the lucky winner of my computer company phone number 347-451-1154 from HBO Marketing where I was an understudy. Let me walk you through it.

We want really big numbers and a logo or certificate. I show my Microsoft Office Specialist logo which will get most jobs done. Put your certificate logo in one layer, text in another layer as shown below.

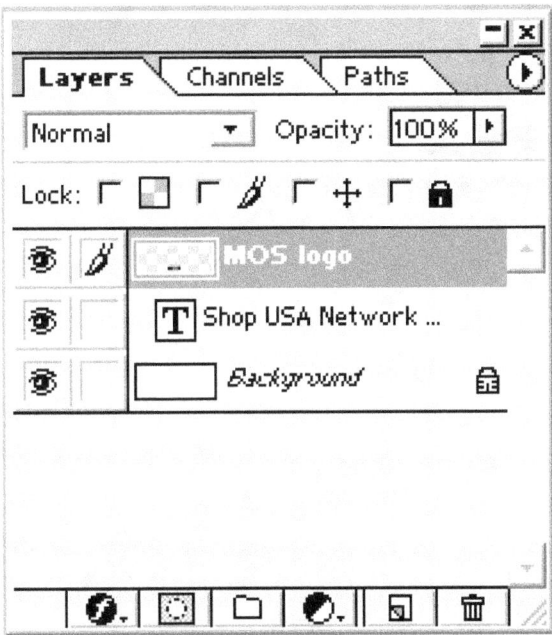

Here is the final piece. A full banner size company piece. Using Adobe Photoshop you can make these as big as you want. One of the reasons that Mac is used over P.C. by design firms that make billboard size banners is Mac computers have memory capabilities way ahead of our time. For the price of one extra memory module upgrade you can have enough memory to make a banner across the entire side of your store or home office.

Shop USA Network Web Site Design

347-451-1154

IT'S ALL COMPUTERS

We are done with everything except for the body text of the web site. We are not going to start from scratch and make our own page layout as there are many pre-made templates available on Microsoft.com Once there, navigate to the Office section of the site or by going straight to Office.Microsoft.com. The templates category will be broken down into made sub-categories, but for our purposes we are going to use either Newsletters or Presentations. Remember, your web site is just a presentation or a newsletter showing off your product. I found a nice text format to use for the home page of my web site and several different formats for the other pages. The templates will include image place holders that will make your job easier. All you will have to do after that is replace the template images with your own and you will be on your way.

Question from the readers: I saved them into .doc format and they could not be used. How do I save my document for the web?

This is one of the most common questions I have from clients and not only in Word but also PowerPoint. You can save your documents for the web. Access has some export database for web features and excel can prepare all kinds of data for a web format.

Click on File/ Save as Web Page. You will be prompted with many choices but choose Web Page. This makes your document and images separate and ready for ftp onto your web hosting service. If you select single file web page your images will be embedded into your document and not always viewable. Simply select web page and choose a separate folder in your documents folder and you are done.

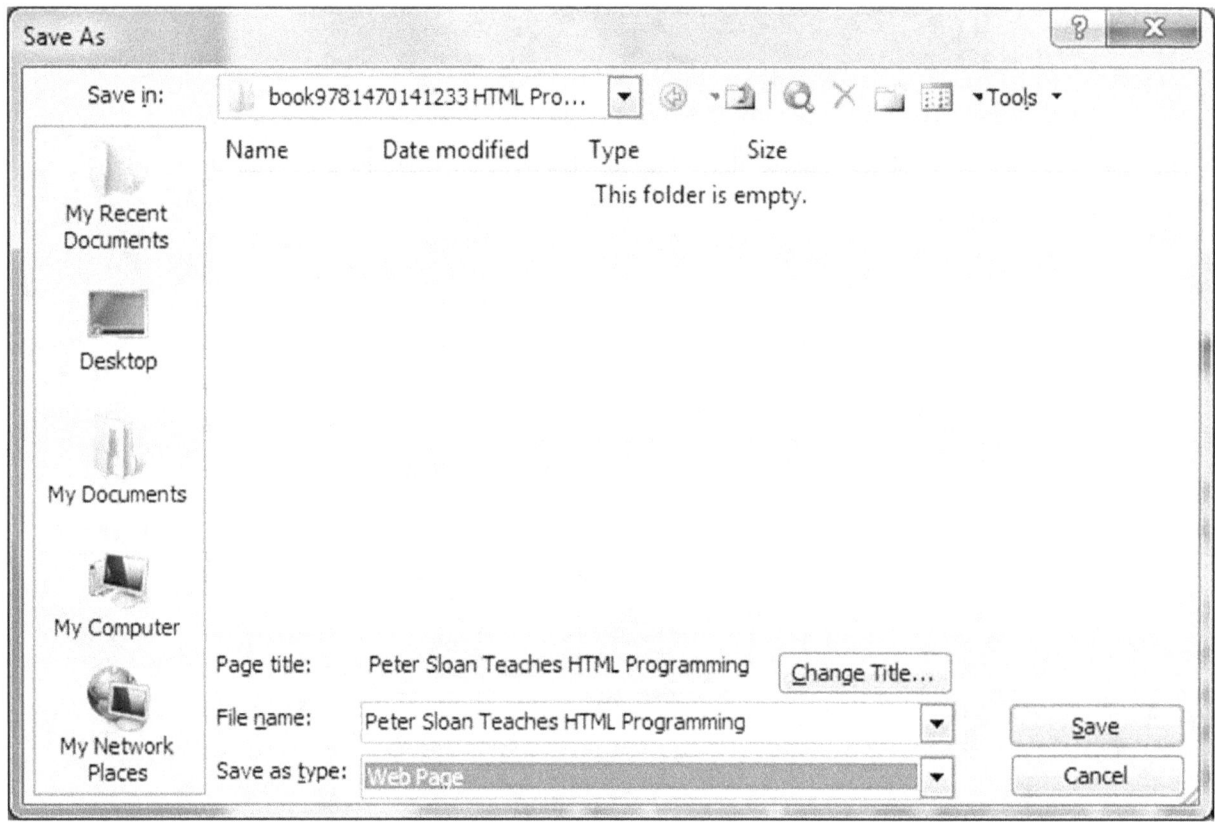

If you look in the top right corner of the Save for Web Page window you will see a Tools button. Click Tools/ Web Options and you will be brought to this screen.

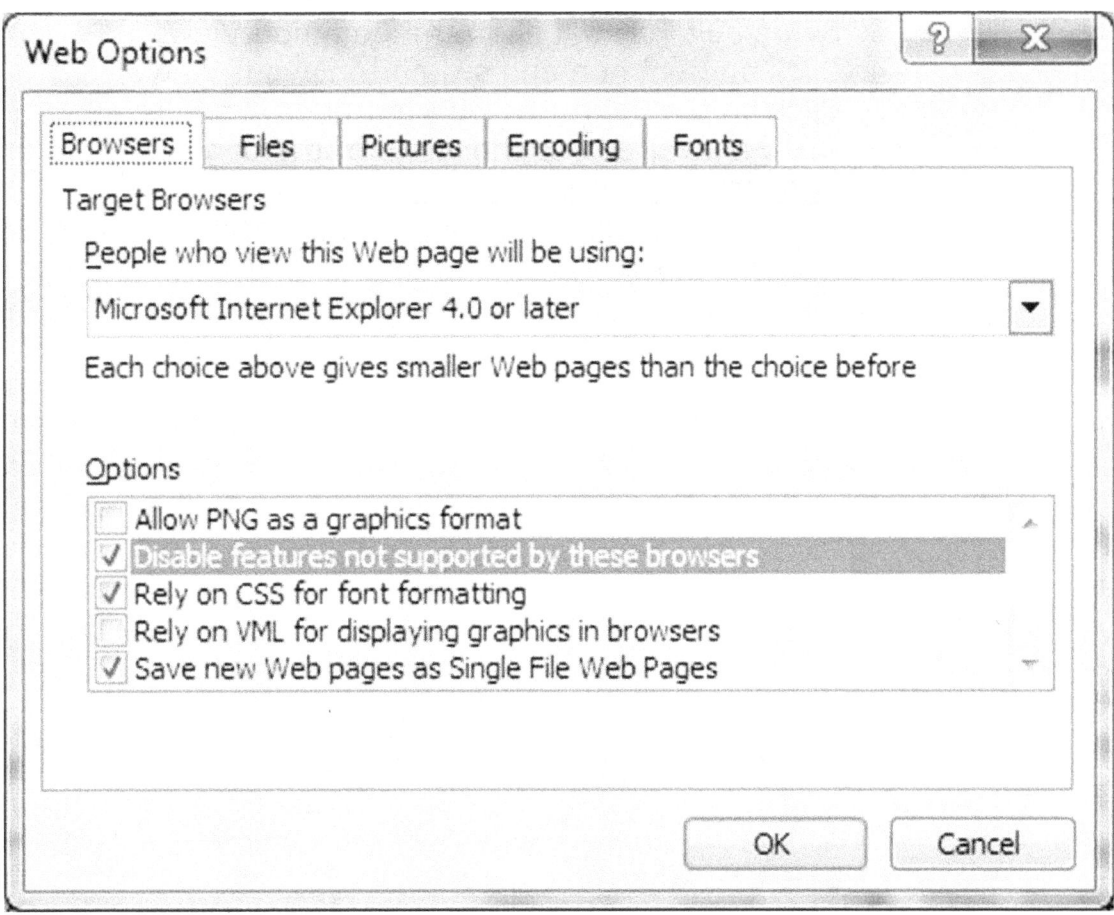

Select you browser options, select image preferences which we will not need to change or change your standard screen size from 800px X 600px to a different size.

Laying out your site in DreamWeaver. You must make your page a fixed 800 pixels width by following these steps.

1. Start DreamWeaver.
2. When the start screen appears click Create New/ HTML.
3. By default you will be in the Common View.
4. Click on Common and switch to Layout View.
5. Click on the light green button titles 'Draw Layer'
6. Draw a layer across the width of the page to approximately the right size of 800px.
7. With your cursor select on the layer and the properties dialogue box will appear.
8. The properties will display one box for Width labeled W change the size to 800.

We are done with making our web document 800px. Go back to the top of the screen which shows Layout View and switch back to Common View.

Now we are going to set up out table to have two columns and a main body on the right with 8 rows on the left. Keep the table width 100%. Add a caption and it is very useful for the readers but they also appear in the search engines.

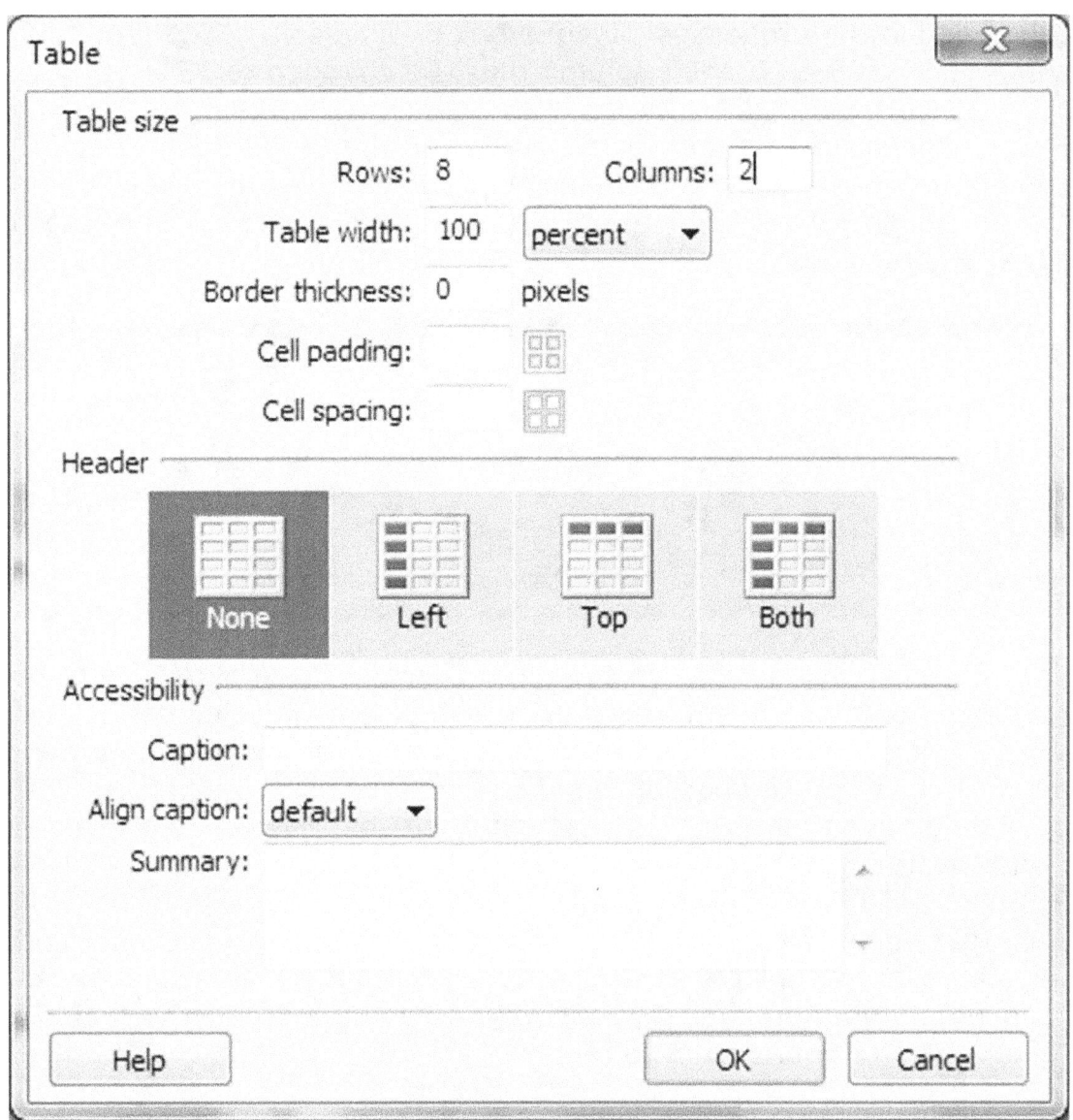

We are going to merge the table cells on the right hand side from the bottom to just one below the top. Click Modify/ Table/ Merge Cells. The tables will be merged and unified as one.

To set the table width, put your mouse cursor in the topmost table portion and in the properties dialogue box it will display 50%. You must change this to 85%. The left column must be changed to 15%.

Follow this diagram to learn how to use the properties inspector. This is one of the most valuable tools in the program. This one single dialogue box can design your entire site, format your text, change your background colors. The list goes on and on.

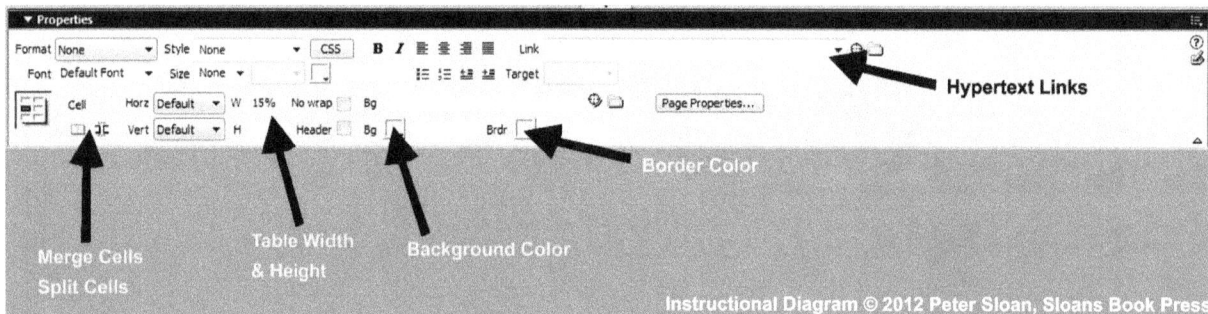

Much like using Word, in DreamWeaver you must click Insert/ Image Browse to the image in your hard drive and insert the selection. If the image appears to be too big, click on the image and the properties window will appear. Click to make your left hand side images all 125 pixels in width, but you should have them set up already in Photoshop, as we went over earlier in this chapter.

That about wraps it up for text and tables. You can get more complex tables built into templates as in Chapter 9, but as far as designing web sites is concerned, your are well on your way to having a productive web site presentation for your clients to read.

Chapter 4: Formatting Your Classified Ad

When I first started on Craigslist, my ad looked just like the other guys, with a long string of words ending with a phone number. There were no images or logos or even color formatted text. I used my special box I purchased years ago of DreamWeaver MX 2004 for the purposes of formatting my classified ad to current day standards. Folks, the bad news is: Microsoft Word saved as a web page and converted into HTML simply is not supported by Craigslist or many other HTML engines. If you are sales-men in the business of making ads it is well worth your investment to buy a copy of DreamWeaver either from Adobe.com or go to your local Staples or J&R Computer store and get a copy right away. While the Adobe Suite costs thousands (and even being a published author I still have not bought one), a copy of the latest version of DreamWeaver in a box will cost you in the $400-500 range and is a license you will use for as many years as you like.

We are going to start with a page of text, format the text, add in the hypertext links, add in our logo and images. Last but not least, our copyright symbol will go at the bottom and your ad will be done. When we are finished you will have an ad ready to be published.

I need to state my name, company name, phone number, availability, certifications just to get started, but also a lot of extra information about what my company does, what our services entail and remember that there is not a limit. Craigslist generally gives one page per customer per week on their site. Your page can have as much information as possible, do not be short and brief like just a fly by night guy from a bad neighborhood. Write up as much about your company as you can for your ad and paste it all together in one large Craigslist advertisement for your readers to see.

Let's get a template. I went to SkillSlate.com and also found templates on Thumbtack.com which is a nice place to run your ad from everything from an artist like myself to an orthodontist looking to book his private doctor's practice with extra clients. There was another service from Expert.io that allowed me to set up telephone consultations for a small fee collected by PayPal. The Expert.io link was not allowed on Craigslist which blocks any links to an online e-commerce platform. Expert.io was later closed down for spamming their e-commerce links across the web were in a free country we do not have the right to ask others for money, (go figure). We will get to that later. You must design a landing page on your web site to be directed from Craigslist and once they are there you can sell them products and services links on a product page with plenty of buy now and other e-commerce links at your disposal, but for now we are getting our classified ad together.

The standard HTML script to make text bigger in size is shown here. It is a script which must be displayed at the top portion of the head of the page. Don't be discouraged; DreamWeaver writes the script automatically.

```
<style type="text/css">
<!--
.style1 {font-size: 18px}
-->
</style>
```

All you need to do to create the script is adjust the point size of the text you are altering. Just highlight the text you would like to change and click on the size and style buttons in the property inspector box and quickly make the changes just like any Word or office document. The <style type> script will be written automatically.

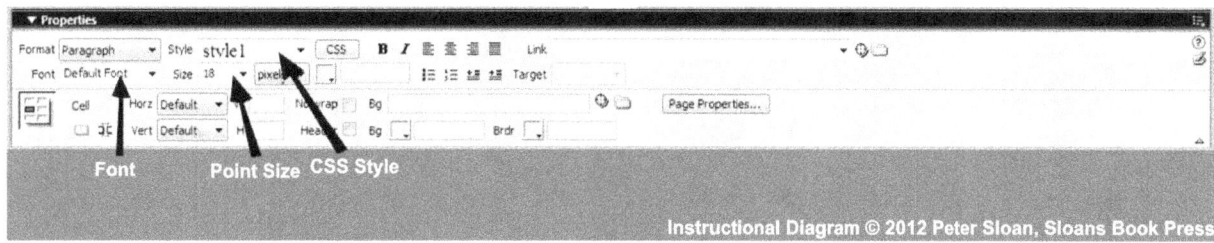

I took years of typographic design classes which always reminded us not to use too many different point sizes on one document. You also want to consider your font. The default system fonts are included but you can click on the 'Font' button and switch from default font or system font to 'Edit Font List'. You will be prompted to browse to a directory where you have your fonts saved. Click on the font you would like to use and click OK.

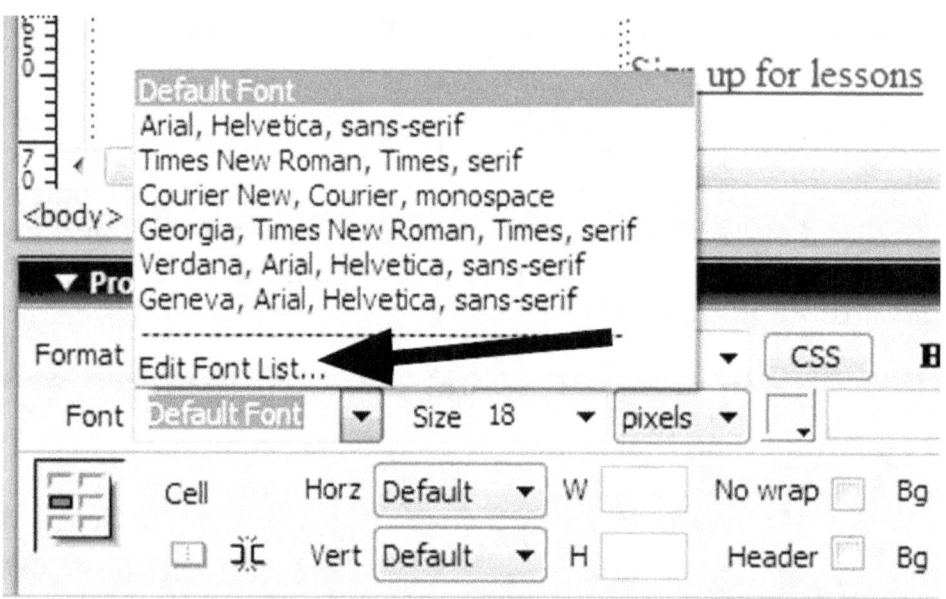

Non-system fonts may not display in your viewers browser and must be embedded. You must purchase a license for your fonts by going to any one of a bunch of sources; I recommend Adobe.com and buying a package of fonts ready to go. You can buy them individually or, if you do not know which font you want buy, an entire package of fonts. Another great place I always found fonts was at Barnes and Noble book stores browsing through the magazine section specifically for computer magazines pertaining to Photoshop and DreamWeaver. Many of the magazines include web sites giving away fonts as well as CD's included for a low price on about 20 bucks plus a coffee; for a real enthusiast that wants to spend a nice afternoon nit picking their web site, this is the only way to go. You won't get the Adobe Suite but you will get some nice take-home recommendations for fonts and plug-ins that would make any web site owner's day.

Inserting images into your classified ad is as easy as upload and copy and paste the HTML code. Let's go through the following steps and get our images ready: after all, we have a classified ad with images and a logo that displays so much better to get the viewer's attention.

1. Create a web hosting or Photo Bucket account
2. Upload your images and logo
3. Copy and paste the code into your classified ad

That is all there is to it. Three easy steps involved to getting your images into your ad. The same three steps are followed to embed a You Tube video which includes a player with a play button. Once you have your images uploaded, your HTML code will look like this...

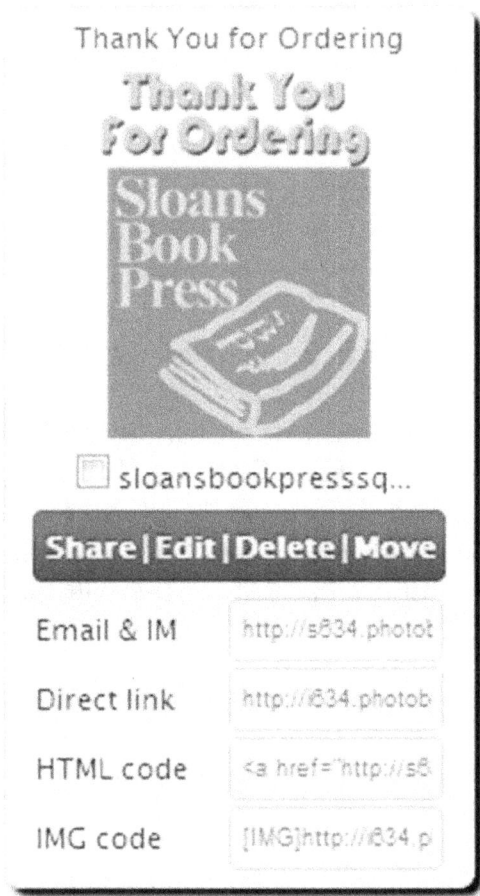

See the HTML code box, simply click with your mouse and select to copy. Paste the code into your DreamWeaver document and you are already done.

Question from the readers: Ok, we copy and pasted our code but it looks like a whole bunch of code numbers, with no image displayed and no one can read it. What did we do wrong?

You copied the code into your design view of DreamWeaver. You must copy your code into the HTML view and the image will be displayed in the preview.

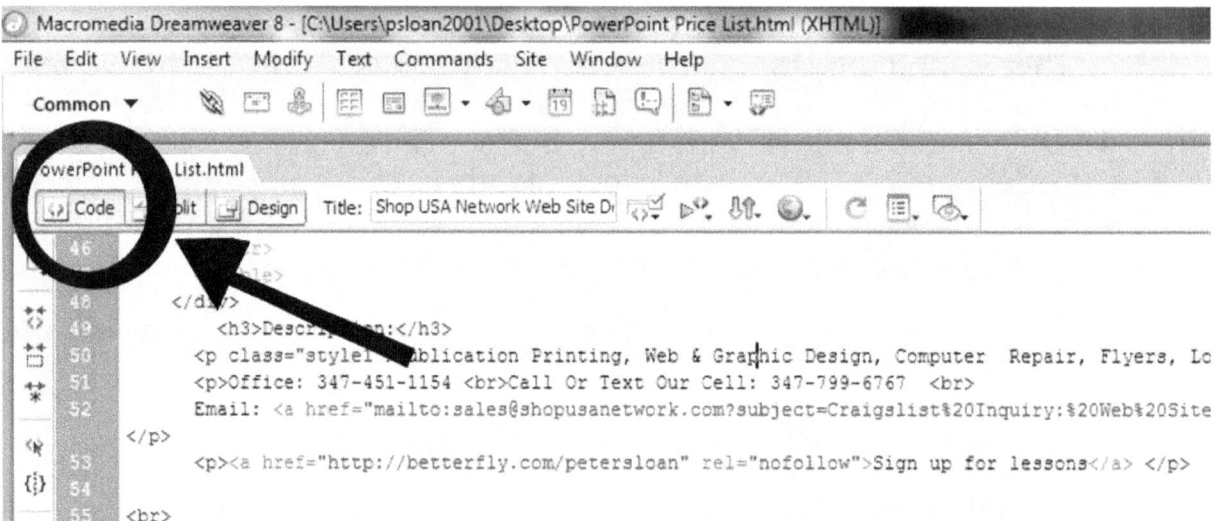

Tip: Copy your code outside of the code brackets. This is a little tricky but code brackets open with a tag and close with another tag. Instead of reading through endless pages of code that no one understands, and having to undo our mistakes simply click on the design view. Click on the design view and then place our cursor where we want the image to go and before, (and I repeat before) copying in the image code, switch to code view and paste into the document where the mouse cursor appears. This will get your image into the right place.

The same goes for embedding your image into a Microsoft Outlook email or GoDaddy email platform. There is an HTML button where you can switch your email from text view to HTML view where you can now copy and paste in your images and self promotion videos.

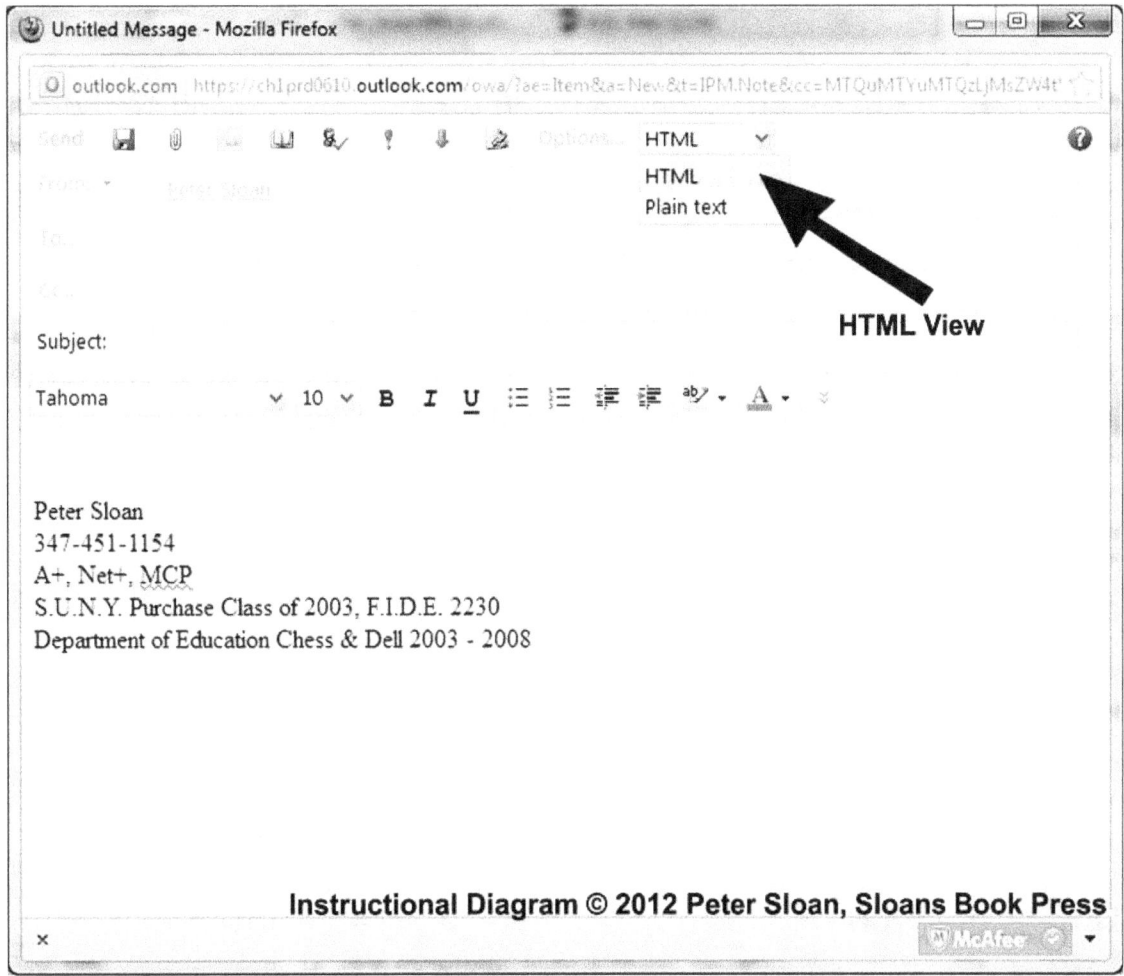

Question from the readers: We have a web hosting account. How do we make HTML links to our uploaded images and get them viewed in our classified ad?

Your images are in a directory for your domain name. Your directory reads like a path from the domain name to the images folder to the name of the image.jpg or .gif. The name of your images folder varies by service and also by what names you gave your directories. A typical path looks like this.

http://www.domainmame.com/images/2012/image.jpg

Test the image link in your browser to make sure it works correctly. If you have the correct directory your image will appear in the top right corner of your Internet Explorer. Once you have a working image link, proceed to the next step.

Question from the readers: So is our image link ready to go? We copy and pasted the link and nothing happened. How do we create the HTML code brackets?

There is one standard code bracket to be used. <img src= followed by the image link and closed brackets. Here is a standard image link for your readers to follow.

<img src="**http://i634.photobucket.com/albums/uu61/comicbooks2009/ shopusanetwork-banner.jpg**" border="0" alt="Photobucket">

The link is created automatically in DreamWeaver by inserting the image link into the properties inspector dialogue box, like we already covered.

Tip: Make your image's link to pages on your web site. You can see one here, <a href="**https://sites.google.com/a/shopusanetwork.com/shopusanetwork**/" target="_blank" rel="nofollow"><img src="**http://i634.photobucket.com/albums/uu61/comicbooks2009/powerpoint399.jpg**" border="0" alt="PowerPoint Web Sites for a Flat Fee 399">

1. Start with the <a href=
2. Followed by the hyperlink to a page on your web site
3. Target _blank keeps your reader on the same page
4. Followed by the image tag we already discussed, <img src=
5. Insert your image link
6. Alt refers to the image title
7. Close the brackets

This is very important. Many of your readers will click on the images and they must have a landing page. On this landing page you can include items for sale and credit card payment links which will be covered later in this book.[1]

---

[1] Editors note: The HTML landing page is key to understanding the content of this book. The end result of the read is the viewer will buy one of our items for sale from our web site and we will make some extra Ca$h.

Chapter 5: Formatting Your Web Site

In the previous chapter we had to upload our images to a third party hosting service to have them display on Craigslist. From this point on we a platform whether it be web hosting or templates to get our web sites displaying properly. There are not that many categories (technical expertise) in formatting web sites. We have the following...

1. Text Formatting
2. Tables
3. Images
4. HTML Links
5. Email Links
6. Other Links such as PDF or PPS
7. E-commerce Links (Covered in Chapter 7)

1. Text Formatting

Like we discussed earlier, Text formatting breaks down much like editing a Word document. Text can be formatted with manual entries such as point size, bold or italic, font, or we can use a shortcut and use styles. In Word this is done by clicking on Format/ Styles and Formatting. A dialogue box appears like the one shown below. You can either use a pre made formatting or create a new style.

The same is true in DreamWeaver, using the properties inspector dialogue box click the CSS button.

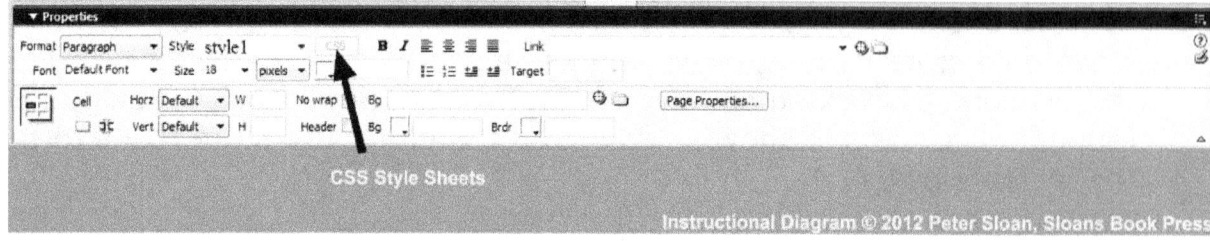

CSS Style Sheets

Instructional Diagram © 2012 Peter Sloan, Sloans Book Press

The CSS properties window will open. There are very few features to learn. Either you are editing a property by double clicking on the field, attaching a new style sheet, creating a new CSS rule, editing a style or deleting a style. Simply play around with the features, double click on options to change the style, add a new property if you want, and you can now add proficiency in CSS and XHTML to your resume. Don't let the job interview get you down.

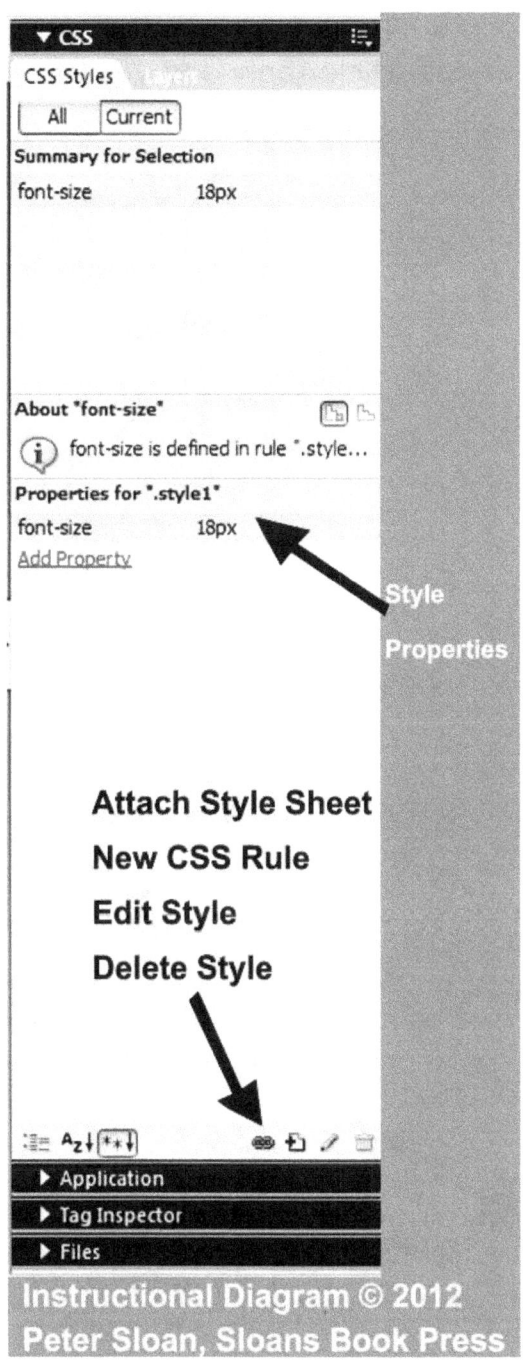

2. Tables

Formatting tables is really easy with Microsoft Word's Table/ Auto Format feature. Select a table you already created like we practiced in Chapter 3, then from the pull-down menu, select Table/ Auto Format and the following dialogue box will appear. Play around with the features to make a nice-looking table. Clicking on the Modify button you can change the font, font character, borders, and colors. If you do not like your changes at the end just click the Default button and everything will reset back to the start. Once you are happy with your changes, click Apply and you are done.

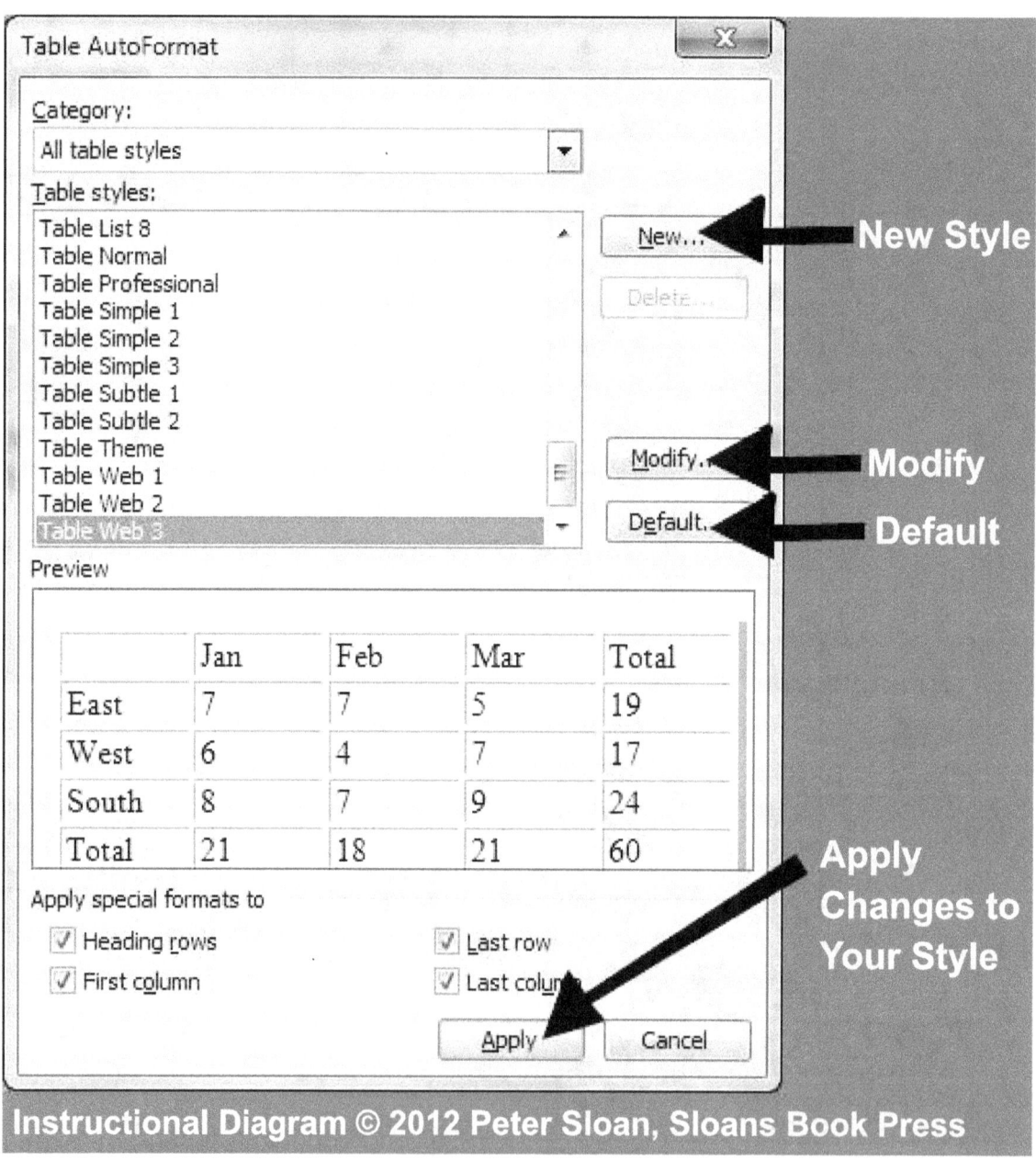

Clicking on Tables and Borders button which appears at the top toolbar gives you a whole wide variety of features such as Draw Table, Eraser, Line Style, Line Weight, Border Color, Outside Border, Shading Color, Insert Table, Merge Cells, Split Cells, Align Top Left, distribute Rows Evenly, distribute Columns Evenly, Table Auto Format as we already discussed, Change Text Direction, Sort Ascending, Sort Descending, Auto Sum which is for spread sheets, Delete Columns, Delete Cells, Auto Fit to Contents, Auto Fit to Window, Fix Column Width, Hide Gridlines and of course reset toolbar to customize which features you prefer to use.

Just play around with it and have a good time customizing your tables. I left my sister with this feature who also is a graduate of art school and she came up with a really nice color scheme with menu features and the works. She refused to show me her techniques, being we have a rivalry all of these years of who is the better artist, but the sky is the limit. Just click on the button and look at the changes and keep at it until you get a result you like and make that your web site.

Tip: Create your tables using Microsoft Word and then later copy and paste them into DreamWeaver.

Question from the readers: We followed your advice and copied our table into DreamWeaver and we lost all of our formatting. How do we keep our formatting from Word to DreamWeaver?

Ok, You forgot to save your word document as a web page. You do not copy from a standard word document. You must click File/ Save as Web Page. Once the document is saved, open the DreamWeaver program and open the saved .htm document. Once the document is open in DreamWeaver, all of your formatting will be intact.

2. Images

Although we already discussed the Adobe Photoshop Save for Web feature and inserting images which is most of the work, there are quite a few features that make the difference between a good picture artist and a web programmer. Your images need to be labeled to appear in the search engines. This is done using either your Photo Bucket account or your web hosting service which will be covered more in Chapter 10: Working With Templates.

Log into your Photo Bucket account and click on an image. You will be taken to a screen that asks for tags. These are what decides how your image will appear in the search engines.

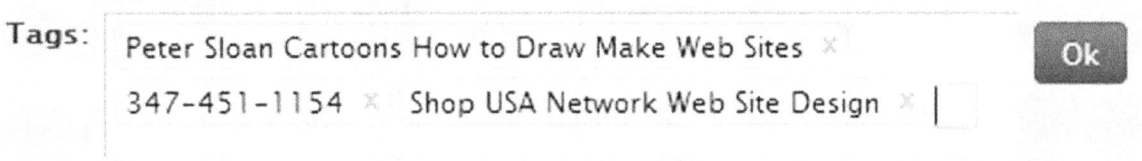

Tip: Spend a lot of time writing and researching your tags. This is the key element to having a web site with a lot of visitors. After you finish making your web page, which can take anywhere from one afternoon to a month not counting revisions, your keywords and tags will put your company at the top of the search engines, where it belongs.

Provided you already own an Adobe license, a very worthwhile investment is a DigiMarc watermark. This can be found by clicking Filter/ Digimarc/ You must get a personalized ID. Click on the personalize button and it will take you to a Digimarc screen to sign up.

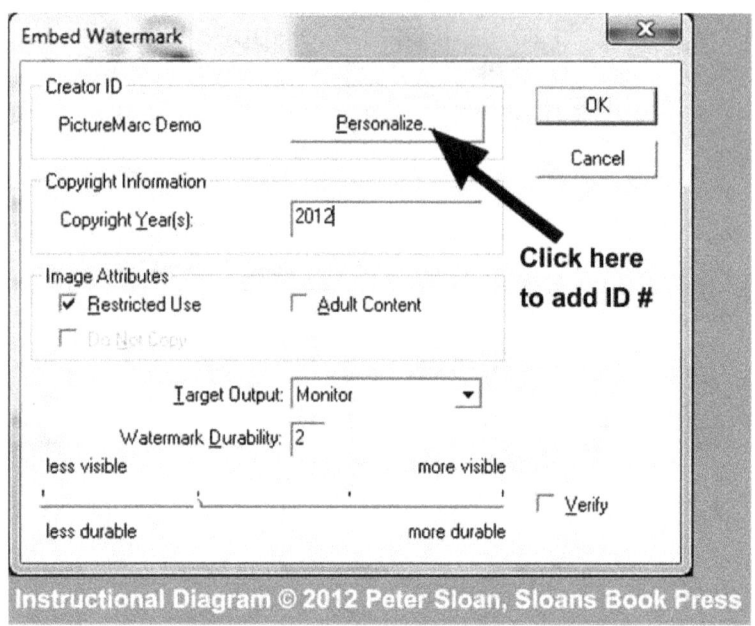

Getting a personalized ID from a company you trust is the only way to go. Do not get involved with some of the less known companies that will offer you $50 watermark tracking for the entire year. Digimarc costs more but this is the most reliable source. The way it works, you add your Digimarc ID to your images and when someone else downloads the photos from your web site and publishes them elsewhere, you can find out who and where. This is done by many companies that retain exclusive rights to all of their images.

My one friend Kevin used watermarks and mailed the infringing parties a letter of demand to pay $100 for the use of the image. This is not my practice and I did not get my books published in Amazon and Barnes and Noble by suing my fans. The more of my work that gets out there, the merrier, but I am an artist and designer. I want people to see my artwork and design.

The exact opposite is true for some advertising firms. It varies by what you are marketing and to whom and for how long. A watermark protects your work from being on the web when you no longer want that particular campaign out there anymore.

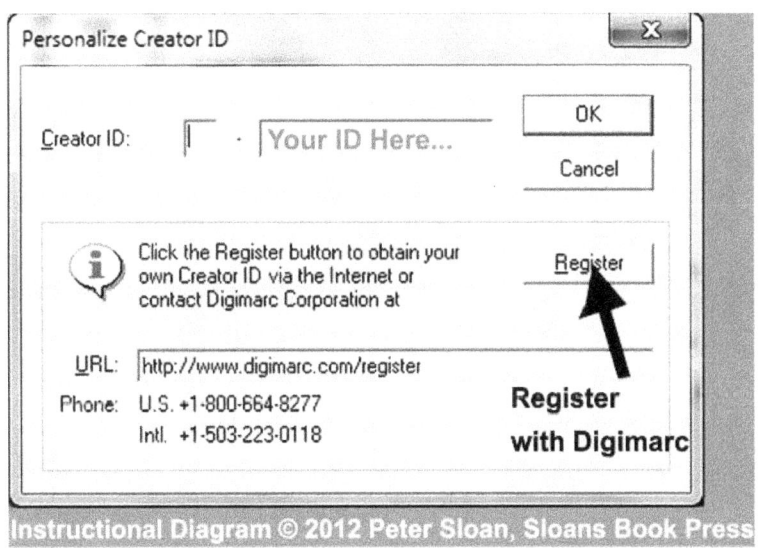

Tip: You can make your web site and watermark copyright and then sell it as a working company. Everything is transferrable except for the Tax ID. Filing copyrights and watermarks to an organizations name is the only way to go these days. It protects your work from being stolen and it protects the owner from a civil lawsuit. Copyrighting by organization is the safest way to go. I met several business people who made a nice living building and selling companies.

File names are recommended to be customized. You want your file names to say either the title of your work or your organization name. Here are two ways to name your files:

As an artist I listed my cartoons with the tag 'Peter Sloan Cartoons' using titles for each individual piece. The file names each with its unique identifier to attract the readers interest.

A more generic approach would be simply labeling all of your images by company name with a number at the end of each one, for example ShopUSANetwork101678.jpg . This keeps your reader on the same page all the time, and you can also label the tags to have the company name as well.

Label your images after a sale or promotion, for example three of my images available in all of the search engines are 575websites3474511154.jpg with my phone number at the end of the extension. Two other labels from this campaign are 399PowerPoint3474511154.jpg and 1299eCommerce3474511154.jpg I added into the tags a detailed description of the services offered for example 575websites3474511154.jpg Having a full break down of what is included for the flat fee which all comes up in a Google search with my copyright registration number also included in the tag.

I worked for a clothing designer that titles all of the shawls for sale in her catalogue first and then labeled each one with an image later. For shawls with more than one image they were given names based on the view. The extra ones were labeled by which color and shade.

4. HTML links

While making HTML links is as easy as clicking Insert/ Hyperlink or in DreamWeaver Insert/ Hyperlink as well, there are quite a number of technical glitches that must be understood.

All the way back, starting out on eBay in 1999, my dad and I both noticed that while our links to our items worked, our links expired after one week and our search links were only viewable on the P.C. and not Mac. Here is an example. As an end result we had to open an eBay store with a store name like http://stores.ebay.com/sloanteaches, which today goes to my Amazon Author page.

Case in point, you have an item you are recommending a customer to buy and you send him this link,

http://www.ebay.com/sch/i.html?_nkw=classics+illustrated+comics&_sacat=63&_odkw=&_osacat=63&_trksid=p3286.c0.m270.l1311

This link is not viewable on the Mac and does not direct straight to an item. We needed a static permanent link that would stay intact for months not to lose customers. We did a little programming homework here and noticed the & symbol and everything after that was what made the link break and, by simply deleting the remainder or the code after the & symbol, the link was now compatible.

http://www.ebay.com/sch/i.html?_nkw=classics+illustrated+comics

This still only solved our problem for search links, but opening our eBay stores and buying our own domain names, remedied the problem and helped our links work better. So here are the categories of links so far...

- Links to items
- Links to searches
- Links to your eBay store
- Links to your domain name

Making a link to an item being virtually impossible and needing to create page where our items can be purchased without deterring our customers, we came up with stores such as eBay pro stores and Yahoo stores. Keeping our store with a static link to buy items that can be published and advertised was my goal, with all of this extra work to get my store working properly. I even had a friend, who scored a job at a Wall Street firm trying to send me some money at one point, asked me what my merchant ID was. Man, we were on the wrong track at this point, giving up on eBay links and moving else where, with a Merchant account money launder our only guess.

Our next guess was email links, but these did not have the ability to take down order numbers or shipping addresses. We needed a computer to record all of the purchases and inquiries for us and not leave our company with credit card numbers that can be tampered or stolen. The Buy Now link was the next best thing and we were on our way to getting our customers the ability to order with ease. More on Buy Now links is covered in Chapter 8: Custom Programming Credit Card Payment Links.

Store links break down into several categories,

- Your home page
- Your store category
- Your company info
- Your product page
- Your TOS and return policy
- Your contact information

My Yahoo store home page is http://www.shopusanetwork.net My other domain name for this business http://www.shopusanetwork.com is more about us with licenses and professional certifications for my readers. This is recommended for any small business to not only reserve the .com but also .net and the .biz will be my Google site which comes free with Google business.

ShopUSANetwork.net has several categories, but I spent an extra year proofing this one campaign for web sites http://shopusanetwork.net/web-site-design.html which spans over several copyrights and was very time consuming.

ShopUSANetwork.net has three web site offers,
1. http://shopusanetwork.net/powerpoint-web-sites.html
2. http://shopusanetwork.net/small-business-web-sites.html
3. http://shopusanetwork.net/ecommerce-web-sites.html

The $200 down payment option has a logistical glitch, where I can price all three buttons at $200 and have my clients pay as they go, which would mean in fact only having one button displayed, for $200 down with three information pages, or one extra button left below for the $200 option. This campaign is still in the making and logistics are never easy, but eventually I will get money coming in to offer some local jobs for a Shop USA Network call center telemarketing campaign.

Multi-media links have gotten much easier since the days of YouTube but we are in the exactly same loop around with some of our links. Links start with the extension http. It is not possible to use the Insert/ Hyperlink feature to embed and tags or codes that start with a bracket such as <. The same goes for any form tags or embed tags; to insert the link you must have an http.

Usable: http://youtu.be/Dgf9sBhTCq8
Not usable: <iframe width="420" height="315" src="http://www.youtube.com/embed/Dgf9sBhTCq8" frameborder="0" allowfullscreen></iframe>

The <tags> are strictly embedded. This is a good example of DreamWeaver suddenly becoming your best friend. Simply place your cursor where you want your video inserted, click the code view and paste in the <iframe embedded code>. While at the moment the YouTube link is not viewable on Craigslist, it is neatly embedded on your website for everyone to view. There are many services that do allow a video to be viewed in your user profile. These days with web sites requiring Face Book login's and easy to share links and files, there are so many to choose from.

5. Email links

Email links are as easy as 123. Using Microsoft Word, Click Insert/ Hyperlink/ and select the Email Address button. In the Text to Display field type the name of the category where this email link is going. In this case, this email link is for my classified ad. I make sure to label each link not to get my inquiries mixed up from the wrong places. The email field always starts with the command mailto: followed by an email address. The subject field starts with what the subject line of Outlook or another email interface will say.

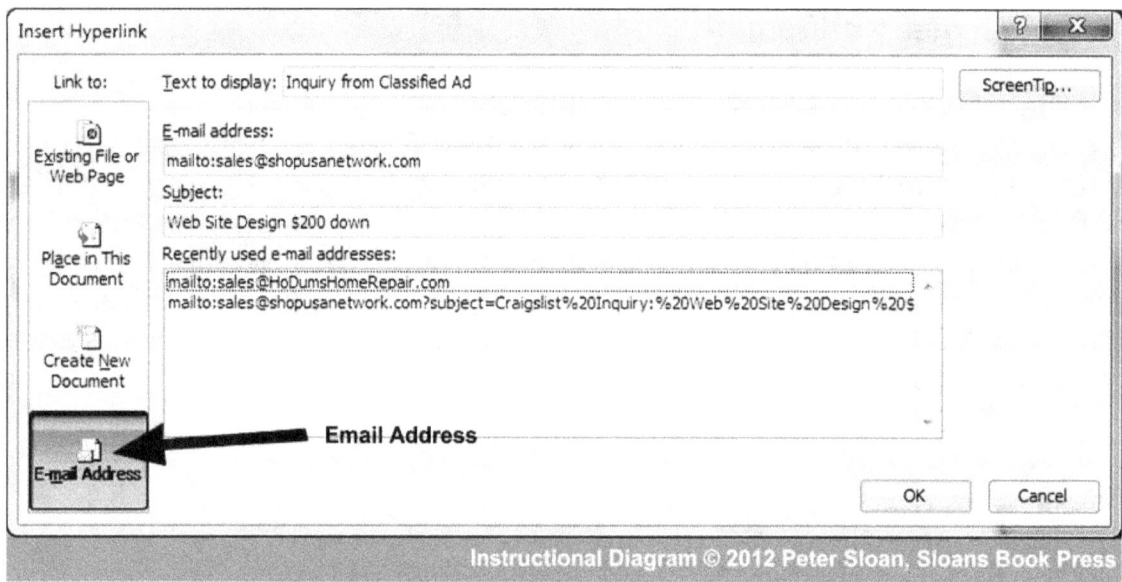

DreamWeaver it is just as easy to make an email link. There is one slight trick where you must manually type the mailto: command to get your emails to shoot out properly otherwise the link will not work. The email link will not have a subject field. For this you will have to use Word.

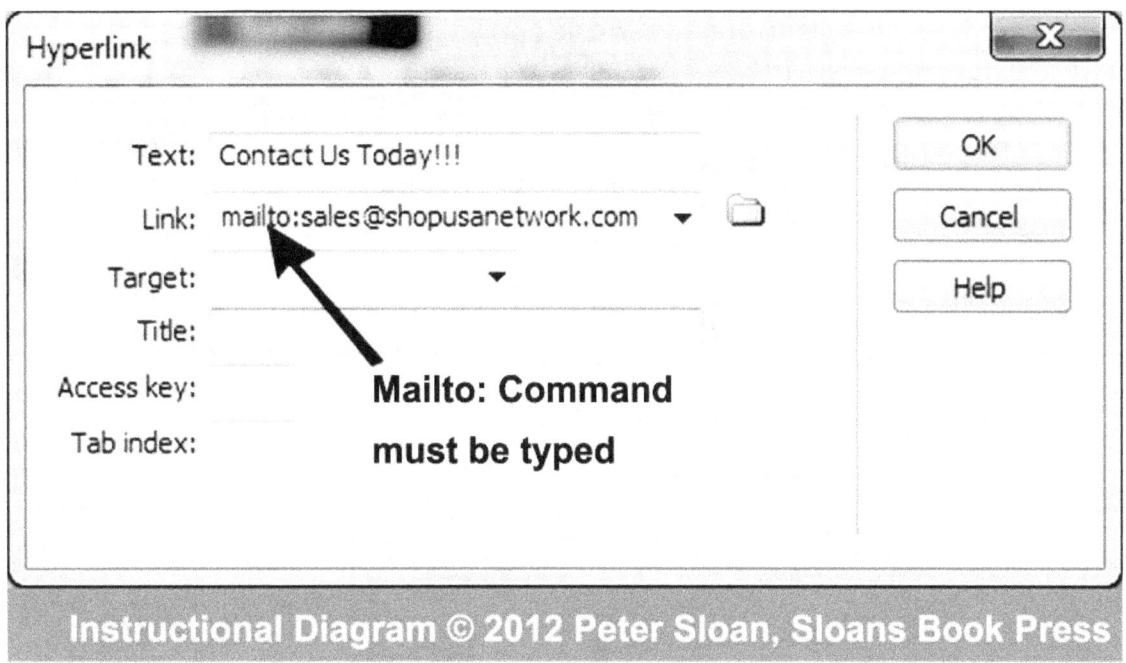

There is one other way to add or edit an email link using the properties inspector box. Once again, you must type in the mailto: command for your link to work. This hyperlink is a monster. I made this link in Word and copy and pasted it into DreamWeaver address field, look here...

mailto:sales@shopusanetwork.com?subject=Craigslist Inquiry: Web Site Design $200 down

This all gets pasted into the properties inspector box shown on the previous page, or in the properties inspector into the Link field.

Skype links are created by simply typing your phone number into your HTML document and the only trick involved is that you must not use a (parenthesis symbol. You must type your number with dashes and no spaces. As long as you have added money to your skype account, your links will work automatically.

Face Book-like links are generated by logging into your Face Book account, creating a new event and accepting new likes. The code must be copy and pasted into DreamWeaver. Your like button will appear automatically.

Twitter links are by extension and do not require any extra programming work. Simply give your party your twitter address and you will be on your way. A twitter address looks like http://www.Twitter.com/nickname

6. Other Links such as PDF or PPS

I have spent enough years on making web sites to quickly pass the PowerPoint certification exam where I discovered what a tool it was to quickly copy and paste all of my links and images from my website to Microsoft PowerPoint and click to either save as a PPS document, which is a PowerPoint Show, which is viewable online on nearly any computer. There are a few tips and tricks to remember before publishing your work for the world to see. You must protect your document done in both Microsoft Word and PowerPoint the same way. Click Tools/ Protect Document. You may also want to register your PowerPoint via a quick easy step of clicking the permissions button, which is located right next to the Save and Open buttons. Once you have a protected PPS file it is ready for the web.

Question from the reader: We made and saved our PowerPoint Show. How do we make a PPS link?

You must upload your document to a web hosting service first, for Microsoft there is nothing better than their online services which are covered in Chapter 9: Working With Templates. The same way you create a link to an image in your ftp directory you create a link to a PDF document but this Microsoft Online services, above and beyond with the options available. Stay tuned for Chapter 10: Working With Templates.

Microsoft Word only requires one click of a mouse to be published as a PDF document. The only trick is you must have a PDF software installed on your system. Once you have your software installed, you just click either Adobe PDF from the top menu or the alternative is to click File/ Print and select Adobe PDF writer from the choice of printers. Once you have created your PDF upload, you document to the documents folder and simply browse with DreamWeaver to the file just the same way you would to create any hyperlink and you will have a working document to display.

Chapter 6: Designing Your Product Page Web Site

A product page web site should only be three to four pages long with your product displayed on the main page with a buy now button, a second page with more detailed sales information and contact information (optional). More on how to create custom credit card payment links is covered in Chapter 8: Custom Programming Credit Card Payment Links. My dad and I always stuck with books and artwork prints which are easy to put in the mail. Including in your mail order a business card or brochure including links to your web site is a great way to get customers coming back. Make sure you ship first class mail or parcel post because media mail does not allow extra notes such as your card.

Here is what your home page should display: a product for sale with all of its information. The one shown below was my first volume in memory of my father who has since passed. I wrote my first book Sam Sloan Teaches A+ for Fathers Day in 2009. The page shows a title, a product image skewed diagonally, a short description, the ISBN and a copyright, including one extra hyperlink to purchase the book.

The other page on a product page site is simply the order form. That is the entire web site, a product and an order form. All of these other components like blog marketing or email marketing do not take place on your web site. All of your emails and blog posting must contain a link to your product page web site, and this is one of the biggest mistakes of my dad in his lifetime was writing a web site with as many crazy articles as wiki leaks but simply did not put product links. To think even with this horrible mistake he died with a quarter of a million dollars in the bank and royalties of over 38K per month paying direct deposit. Here is a sample credit card order page that appeals to customers.

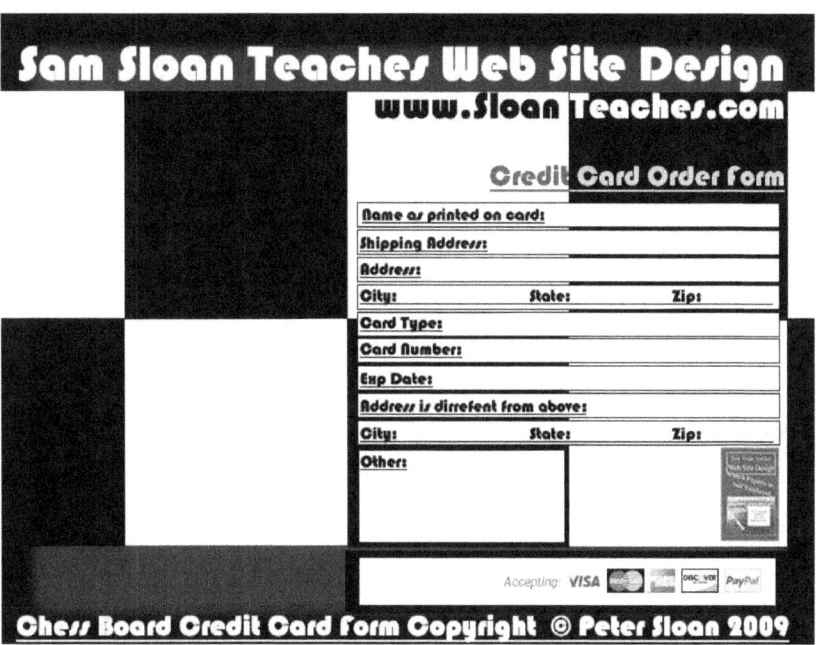

One fine point is the phone number. I do not sell books over the phone but my friend and teacher all these years, Sharif, owns an electronics store and posts his number in big digits for everyone to read the size of a billboard. I looked around and found many car companies and real estate agencies doing the same. A well-composed phone billboard can make your business tons of money. Here is one in a smaller scale but I display the logo of my Microsoft certification and my company name and slogan.

How you approach the contact information is up to you, and it really depends on what kind of business you have, but with the earning potential of credit card payment links, it does not make sense to just have a web site that only takes new client leads but does not accept payments. Everyone must have a product, even if it be your legal notes on DVD (as my dad often published not having other content), or a real estate broker could really use a nice periodical of listings printed and mailed to clients for a small fee aside from her income broking apartments which changes month to month. I even met some construction workers who told me they only sell construction liens online but I got them started on manuals and floor plans they can reproduce and sell for credit card cash. It is up to you and there is no deadline to publish your work in our free 50 states of the U.S.A., but time is money and there is no reason to wait around.

Chapter 7: HTML Formatting Your Blog

Like we covered briefly in the previous chapter, inserting product links into your blog posting there is a little more to it. A nice blog posting will have images, formatted text as well as associate links.

So we have our ad posted on the blog as follows:

Ho Dums, Licensed Contractors. Order a guide book for $8.99 plus shipping Satisfaction Guaranteed. CLICK HERE

Now that is not enough. A blog posting should have a rhythm and display your link several times. You want to build up more attention while your reader scrolls down the page. How is this one for a better fit?

Ho Dums, Licensed Contractors at your service. We have been contracting for over 10 years and can get your interiors done for a great price. Order a guide book for $8.99 plus shipping Satisfaction Guaranteed. CLICK HERE

You order from the other guys and got unfinished jobs and overpriced bills, our contractors work for a fixed rate and you can view our prices by ordering one of our guide books for $8.99 plus shipping CLICK HERE

A survey of our clients said not only did we get the job done but we saved them money and left them with a nicer property. You can't get the quote over the phone or by email, you must order one of our guide books for $8.99 plus shipping CLICK HERE

Now you have gotten in your link several times and have driven some extra interest to your ad. You need to add in some images. Going back to Chapter 5, you need a image hosting service such as GoDaddy or Photo Bucket to host your image and even then, not all blogs will accept your html code. These days many of the editors have a text view and an html view where you can see a preview of your embedded code before you click the submit button, and we all know how important a preview is for that really important promotion or sale that you want just right. The blog I always recommend is Blogger or Blog Spot which is really easy to customize. The blog is not public and you have to invite your own friends to build a list, but it is great to customize and make your postings look better.

Associate links are a great way to make money online and can potentially get millions of clicks in one day, if advertised correctly. I know, a lot of these guys have ad's running to make $175,000, while you sleep and our links never get clicks, but there is a little more to it in terms of paying for advertising such as Search Engine Optimization. Getting your blog formatted correctly from the start and then advertising in the search engines is one of the best ways to get tons of extra business. You must set up every nook and cranny before putting your ad out there for millions to see. I ordered my Search Engine Optimization just this month and that was after having my books published for over two years, but I did not have a complete that showed consistency. I waited until I got enough extra blog exposure, set up all of my associate links as an author and then finally ordered the SEO and I still have a few more weeks until it is active. Following over all of the areas we are covering in this books up to this point to format your ads and websites, and we get to the next and best chapter...

Chapter 8: Custom Programming Credit Card Payment Links

Credit card payment links are as easy as making Photo Bucket image links these days. We are going over a few easy steps to fill out a form and then all you have to do is copy and paste into your site.

Go to your PayPal account and click on Merchant Services. There will be several options to choose but we are creating a payment button.

- Choose the button type, but Buy Now is recommended
- Type in your item name
- Make an item id, which is not a mandatory field but it helps organize your store better
- Set your price and choose a currency
- Drop down menus with price are for items with multiple prices for example one chess piece key chain $5, 3 for $12
- Drop down menu for an extra field such as a size or color
- A text field where your customer can type in text
- Shipping
- Sales tax rate as we discussed earlier how to get a Tax ID
- Security settings

There is an entire second section of setting up the buttons for inventory such as setting the quantity of how many items you have in stock and track profit and loss.

Customizing advanced features such as a 'Thank You For Ordering' page and a 'Out Of Stock' page.

Once you are done, you will simply click 'Create Button' and the next page will allow you to copy and paste the code into your DreamWeaver's html view. You will have a nice, neat Buy Now button for all your readers to purchase your items.

There are other payment providers. I recently noticed Amazon not only has payments but you can create Amazon Buy Now buttons. I never use mine because I have all my books with Amazon and don't want a customer complaint with a negative balance to close my account overdraft but that is just me. I keep all the bad sauce in PayPal where it belongs. Heck, if Amazon ever noticed that I have refunds from Baseball greats like Mr. Bautista over a San Francisco – N.Y. Giants 2011 negative of $2,005, my boss might flip, but as long as the two companies never talk!

You can also get a merchant account at your local bank and this is the old fashioned way to do business. PayPal has only been around since 1998 but the banks have been processing payments for merchants for much longer. The banks are much stricter about opening these accounts than PayPal and you will need a lot more material such as a Business Certificate, a Registered Corporation, Your Business Tax Returns, maybe even qualify on a business credit card first. Good luck with getting approved. Not everyone does because you have to understand they are leaving themselves open to a chance you can swipe cards and leave a negative 65K and they are stuck with the bill. I had a PayPal account for over 10 years before I started with business banking and all of those PayPal commissions you pay go on your merchant credit rating so don't curse the skies when PayPal charges you 2.3% Think of it is an investment in your future.

Chapter 9: Building Templates

For the purposes of this chapter we could not use Microsoft or screen shots for copyright reasons but we will go over step by step how to create these web sites from a template.

Create an Office 365 account at www.Office365.com Transfer in your domain name and add users and email for your Outlook. We are going to focus on your web site.

- Click on Website

- Click on Home to be taken to your main page

- Click on the top and customize your header

- Select the design tab for more options on page formats

- Click on the body of the page and insert your text

- To add HTML code from PayPal or Amazon Associates click insert HTML. A dialogue box will appear, copy and paste in your HTML and you also have an option at add images and links

- To format your text click Home, select your text and use the formatting features the same as using Microsoft Word

- To insert a slide show place your cursor where you would like the slide show to be, click Slide Show and a dialogue box will appear and your images will appear. If you have not yet uploaded your images, click on Save and Publish and then click Close Web Page. You will be brought back to the Website pages directory. On the left hand side click Images and you will be prompted to upload each image one at a time

- Make sure to include tags, Click Upload Picture. You will be brought to a directory where you can browse to a picture to display. Once your image appears, scroll down and you will see the following fields, with a title, date, a description that will appear in the search engines as well as the keywords. It is critical to label each and every image. This is how many web sites get most of there traffic

- Go back to web pages, click on your home page, click Home and then click New Page. A dialogue box will appear to label your page with a title as well as the extension for the file. You can choose to make the page a parent or a directory located within a page

- Click Insert Table, select a style, color and choose the number of rows and columns

- Click Insert Video, now while you can use HTML, You Tube is what everyone is talking about. To get a link in You Tube click share, the link starting http://youtu.be/ will not work. You use the url in your browser that starts with http://www.youtube.com/watch?v= and click preview and your video will display. Click ok and save the changes

- Click Contact Us to insert a form. A dialogue box will appear only asking for your business email. Click ok and you are done you have a contact form already

- If you click on More Gadgets you will find an extra feature for PayPal links although you can insert them into HTML and also some other features such as stocks, weather and maps

- The design features are very vast and complicated. You can select a style for your header, under themes you can find hundreds of different themes to choose from

- Design Location decides weather your web site reads horizontally or vertically

- Clicking Hierarchy you can change the order of your pages in the navigation scheme. By clicking on items with sub items on the left side you can rearrange those as well

- Format does background colors

- Layout decides how many panes the body of your document has. This does not affect the header or the navigation, but only the body of the web page

- CSS is a great reason to have already purchased DreamWeaver. You can simply make your style sheets and then copy and paste the CSS code. It is better to customize them in DreamWeaver first and then get them over to Office 365 later

- Setup decides your page size and you can add a search box later

- Footer is a good place to insert extra links to other sites as well as your copyright code

Now go back to the main control panel by clicking Save and Close. Once you have a document, you really like the way the format looks, click the check box on the side of the template and click Save as Template. The template will be saved into the templates folder. Templates take a lot of work to make and a lot of hours. Once you have your page just the way you want it, click on make sure to preserve the document the best you can.

What is really neat is all of the above templates can be simply copy and pasted into Word and saved for a different software. While word at 8.5 X 11, it is not the right page size for the internet you can click. View, Web Layout and then you will see the entire document as a web page. To save it correctly click on File, Save as Web Page and when the prompt comes up it will automatically be in HTML format. This file format is ready for the web and to be uploaded to a service like GoDaddy at any time.

Microsoft is just one template building service. There are many. GoDaddy currently has Web Sites Tonight for a modest fee. Yahoo comes with a page builder as so does 1 Plus 1 and many other services. If you would like to browse around, just get a copy of Web Site Magazine and browse around for a service you like, but take it from me. I have the best hands on technical art training in making web sites that is on the market today. I used to make my web sites from scratch in DreamWeaver and would get such a head ache from customers complaining that everything was not perfect. I would have to work tooth and nail on different size changes and minor errors in formatting. Microsoft's templates made my life so much easier. Instead of having customers screaming on the phone demanding changes to tables over again, I instead got immediate compliments. I also got referrals right away asking for one of these sites they could make in a few weeks and have since then become a web design tutor. These template building softwares are so easy to use that you can teach a 90-year-old lady how to who cannot even turn on her optical mouse. Say what, an optical mouse is always turned on but that's right, the old lady couldn't figure it out; now she is making web sites every day and trying to get certified as a Microsoft Office Specialist. As long as she works with office software every day, she is sure to pass.

Chapter 10: Adobe Photoshop Graphics

We are going to do one short and simple exercise in circle square triangle putting each object on its own layer and rearranging the layers in the layers window. To finish off, we will save the image as a gif with a transparent background.

We will draw a square. Select the Rectangular Marquee.

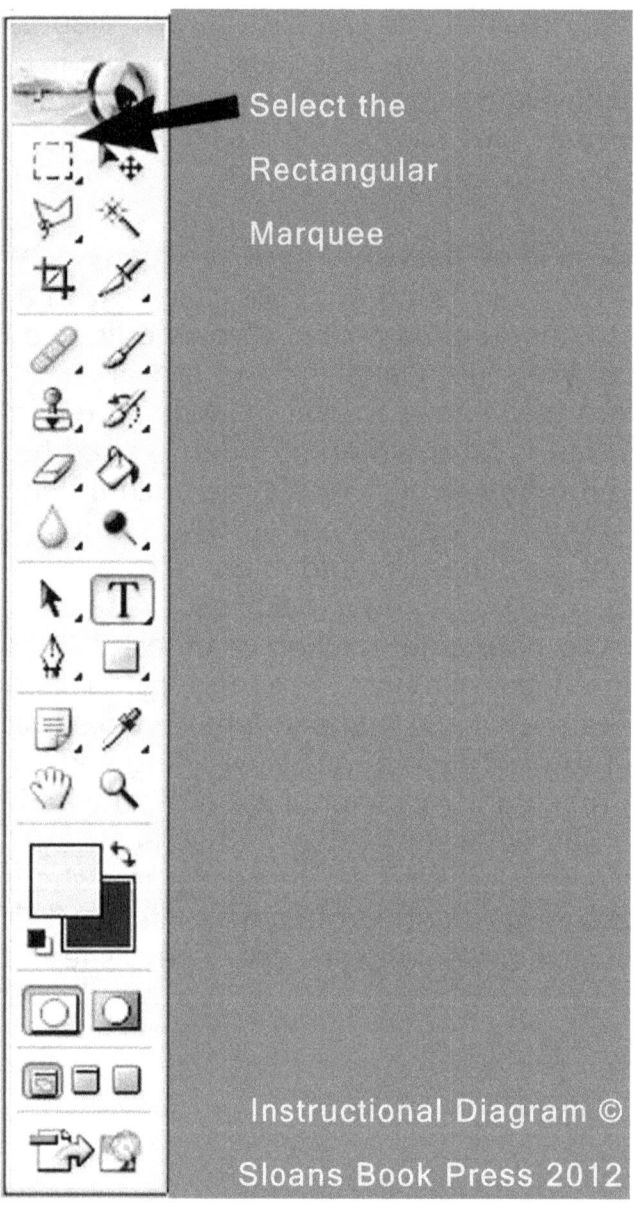

Select the Rectangular Marquee

Click File, New to create a new document. Give the document a name. Decide on a width and height. Make the resolution 72 dpi for web images. Set the mode as RGB. Set the background to transparent.

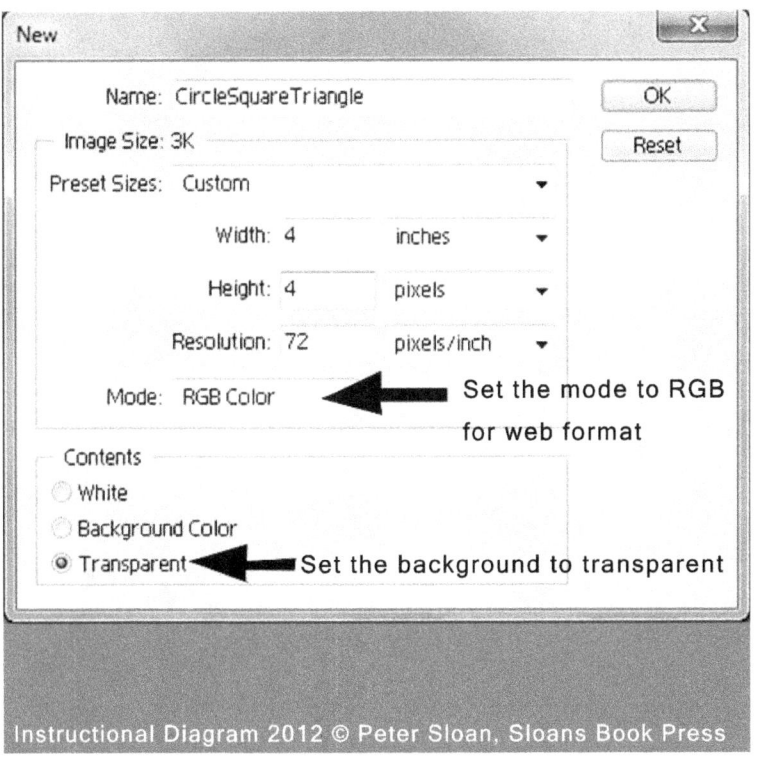

Hold down the shift key with one hand and click and drag your selection tool over the canvas to get the shape of a perfect square.

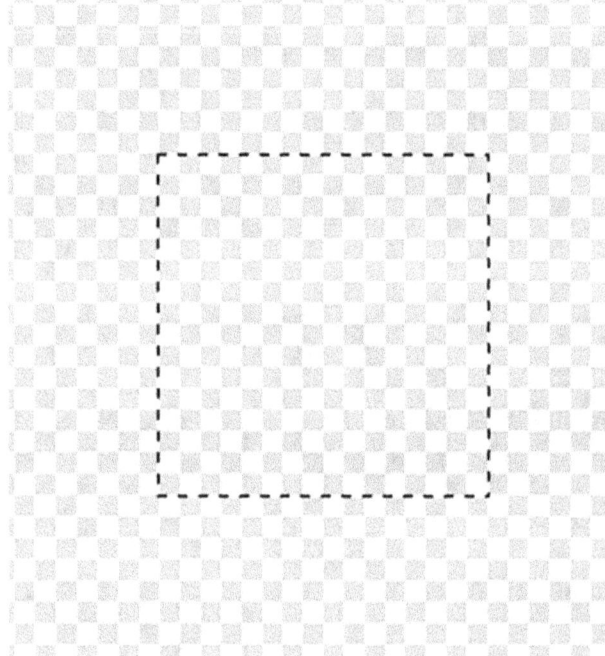

Select the paint bucket tool.

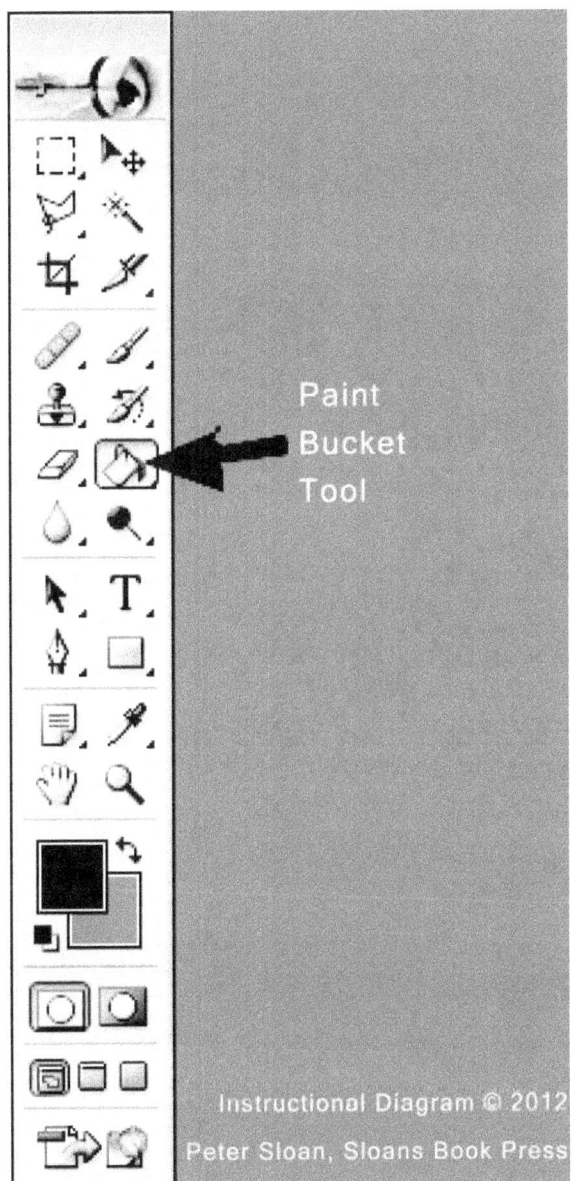

Paint
Bucket
Tool

Next, choose a color. The colors I recommend for this assignment are Blue, Red and Yellow.

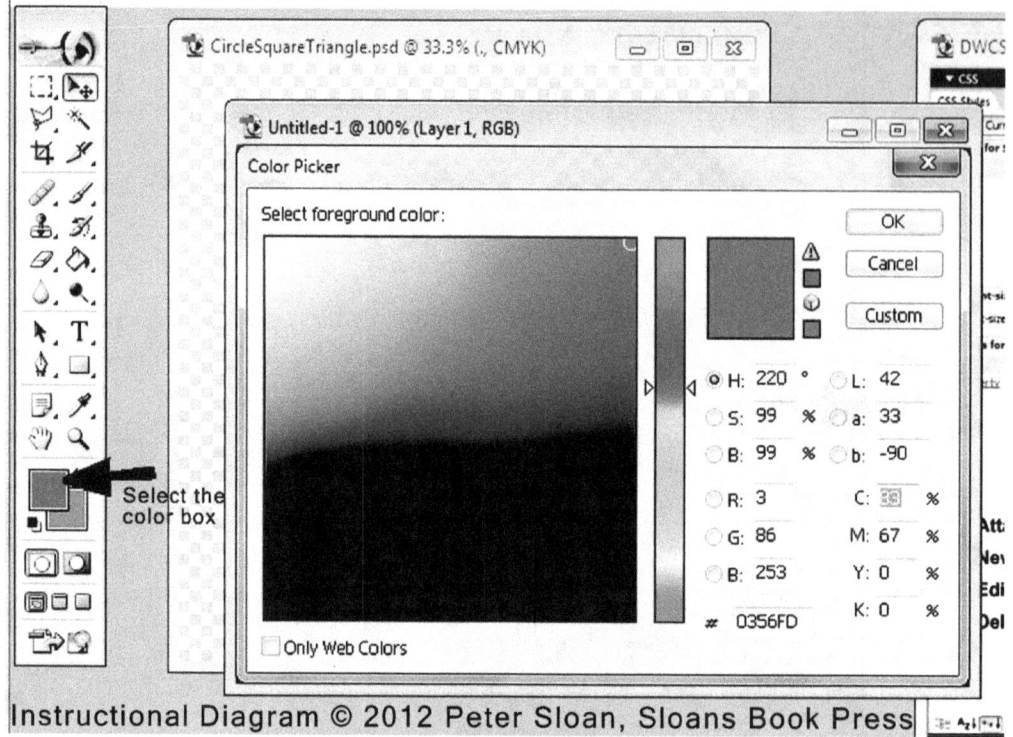

Instructional Diagram © 2012 Peter Sloan, Sloans Book Press

Use the paint bucket tool to fill in the square blue. Congratulations. You got through these steps so far. You have created a perfect square in Photoshop.

Now we are going to create a layer. After this the task will be much easier and we will be repeating the same steps to create the circle and triangle.

Click from the pull down menu select Layer, New Layer. Name the layer 'Circle'. Now we will use the Circular Marquee.

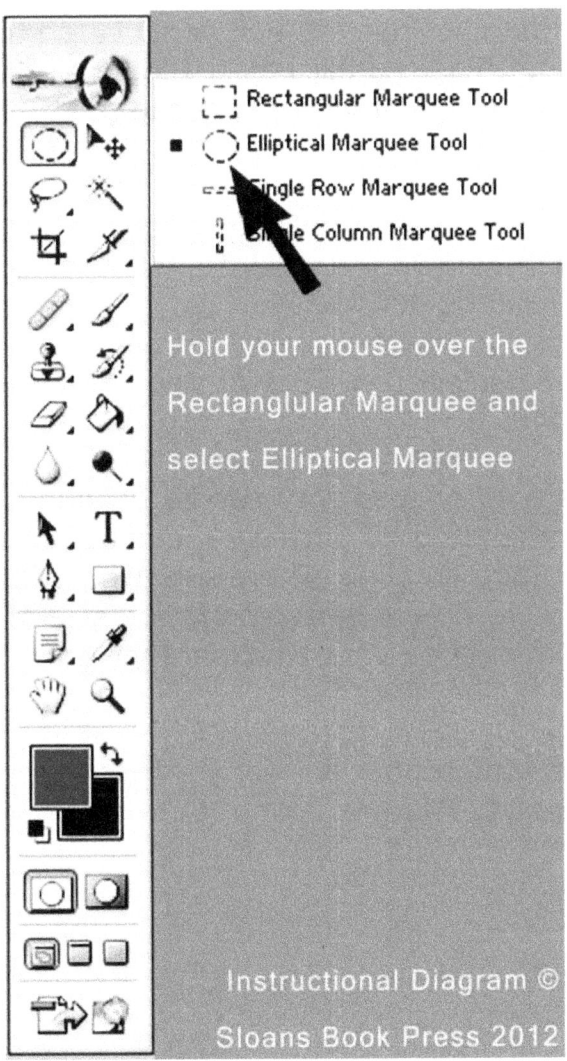

Rectangular Marquee Tool

Elliptical Marquee Tool

Single Row Marquee Tool

Single Column Marquee Tool

Hold your mouse over the Rectanglular Marquee and select Elliptical Marquee

Instructional Diagram ©

Sloans Book Press 2012

Follow the same procedure as drawing the square shape, and with your left hand hold down the shift key and with your right hand click and drag to make the circular selection.

Click on the paint bucket tool, and then use the color picker to select the color yellow.

Click with the paint bucket tool within the selection to fill the circle with the selected color. The circle is complete.

Once again create a new layer using Layer, New Layer and give it the name Triangle. For this step you will need to use the Polygonal Lasso tool. It is located right below the selection tool. The regular Lasso Tool is selected by default so you will need to hold down the cursor and choose the Polygonal Lasso tool.

You make a shape with the Polygon Lasso tool simply by clicking on different areas around the page. When you want to finalize, your selection simply double click and the selection will be defined.

Click on the color picker tool and select red. Click on the paint bucket to fill in the selection and you are done.

We must save the selection as a gif or jpeg so it can be used in web format. For this exercise I am recommending gif because jpegs do not have transparent backgrounds. Click File, Save for Web. There are two options for file type. You can also change the image simply by typing in the size of the pixels and clicking apply. You can also change your transparency and a few other features.

This is a great exercise, by the way, taught by many art teachers in schools all over the world. Circle, Square, Triangle is one to remember. Make sure you practice all the time.

Chapter 11: Copyright, Logos And Trademarks

Copyrights are a lot easier to file than back in the old days. A quick visit to www.Copyright.gov and register with a user name a and password. There are a few simple rules to follow. Copyrights for web sites generally consist of only text and images, and once in a while an MP3. I know some people who build code from scratch using DreamWeaver and copyright their HTML code which is useful for programmers, but HTML code is very generic and there is very little room for original authoring. All the big company web sites use APS software to make churn out web sites like a cookie cutter. If you ever are fortunate to get involved in classes where you can design software and file for your own patent, jump at the opportunity. Starting with a bachelors in computer science with a specialty in C++ is the route and it is very many years of classes before you can even program a working interface with limited scope never mind a web site generating software. These big companies hire programmers and pay them hundreds of thousands per year to write a new interface. We all know the story of Bill Gates founding Microsoft with stolen code, but that is from the story books. Software engineering is the work of an entire firm and not cheap to finance, and most of them do not take off like a pie in the sky. Sticking with a sales campaign of web sites, email marketing and SEO with a working merchant account and a business phone, you can make your work at home job a 120K per year enterprise.

Your text and images must be copyrighted. Remember only a few pointers. Do not try and copyright someone else's images. They must be the property of your company. Do not file copyrights of work you did as a freelance for someone else. Those are called work for hire and when you were paid by the hour you forfeited your rights. If you copyright under an organization name, make sure you own it and have proof ready, but basically as long as your work is original, you will not have a problem. The only time I had to change a copyright is when I left it on my chess artwork web site for over two years and someone wrote me to take it down. It was in fact a very large graphics card company and I was honored to be chosen as a good artist but most business people would not feel the same. Contracts for employees to work for hire you can get from an attorney. They are very common and ever attorney has some available.

Logos are what identify the work of your company. When you copyright your logo, I would recommend making a separate copyright fee to put your logo in its own registration number for $35 extra. Then again the way I do it is copyright each new work with a logo and each time I submit the logo I change the colors. Each new copyright does not use the same artwork as the previous. My dad is a very old fashioned person and refers to his copyright as his seal like it is from a court. Anyone that infringes on my dad's logo gets a letter to remove it immediately or he takes down their whole web site by complaining to the authorities. I never thought that I should complain about my artwork being used by another web site because I am from a long line of art schools, Universities and Institutions that all teach the same thing. You cannot ever get famous unless you get your work out there.

As a friend of mine who works on Wall Street explained to me many years ago, you can hear the most rigorous legal explanation of why trademarks are only for large corporations but anyone with a series of work in conjunction like this books series; for example, 'Sloan Teaches Book Series' is a trademark of my company 'Sloans Book Press'. Another example of a trademark is Windows. While Microsoft is Bill Gates Corporation, his trademark is the Microsoft Windows Operating Systems of which there are many now. Of course Microsoft has many and you can read through their IT notes and services on their web site www.Microsoft.com It is that simple. The actual components of the operating systems, are patent protected, for example all of the code used to write the .ini and .sys files.

I had my own attorney threaten me when I asked him if I should write some of these computer companies a letter saying I made them a really nice advertising piece and if they could be so kind as to make an optional payment but he warned me that I am not providing any advertising service but I dare infringe on a trade mark. For the holidays I am mailing my attorney a free copy of the Art Market Guide 2012, for reasons that printed material at the book store is clearly an advertising service and the recommended amount to ask for is between $25-75K A few years from now I will hopefully have a contract to mail out for a client to sign. There are a few things in the mix such as that the first question a company will ask is 'How Many Sold' 'How Big Is The Exposure' but it is only my first two years with my published book series and book companies got smarter paying their bills first, employees and stockholders second and the authors later. It is called accruing royalties and this does not happen over night. It is the old days that book stores like Borders paid $3.8 Million as an up front advance and then find out none sold and today they are out of business. It just takes time.

Chapter 12: Bang You Are Done, Fully Operational Business, A Few Tips And Things To Watch Out For, Scam Alerts And Fraud

Advisory, Watch out for any transactions asking for Western Union.

That is one to look out for, but I took a whole class with American Express Merchant Accounts and there is a lot more to it than that. Don't take any order from anonymous emails. Do not accept any third party check, especially if the individual tries to pay with a company check. Because our business is mostly over the phone and online, I recommend taking this fraud protection class. According to American Express, every $100 of a chargeback costs the business $300 in losses.

Watch out for parties that request your PayPal email. If they order a service, take down their order and send them an invoice. If the client completes the invoice you are paid. These professional thieves will try and find out your PayPal email address just to be able to follow your store and send spoofing payments. It looks like money available in your account, but after a week or even two months suddenly your balance goes negative and your customer runs away with all of the merchandise and sometimes even cash. Look out for any spam emails pretending to try and buy your car, or give you a gasoline check from a company you never heard of. Do not take any transactions from web sites with an extension from Russia. Even if you get a payment our banks cannot except money from there banks. These will almost always result in a bounced check fee and maybe severing relations with your bank.

But with all that being said, best of luck. Most likely you will just type up some scripts and copyrights and have an immediate sales appeal and make a bundle of money.

Peter Sloan
A+, Net+, MCP
S.U.N.Y. Purchase Class of 2003, F.I.D.E. 2230
Department of education Chess & Dell 2003 – 2008